ELIZABETHAN CROSS STITCH

BARBARA HAMMET

David & Charles

A DAVID & CHARLES BOOK

David & Charles is a subsidiary of F&W (UK) Ltd.,
an F&W Publications Inc. company

First published in the UK in 2004

Distributed in North America
by F&W Publications, Inc.
4700 East Galbraith Road
Cincinnati, OH 45236
1-800-289-0963

A catalogue record for this book is available from the
British Library.

ISBN 0 7153 1630 3

Executive Editor Cheryl Brown
Editor Jennifer Proverbs
Art Editor Prudence Rogers
Senior Designer Lisa Forrester
Production Controller Ros Napper
Project Editor Lin Clements
Photography Kim Sayer and Karl Adamson

Printed in Singapore by KHL Printing Co Pte Ltd
for David & Charles
Brunel House   Newton Abbot   Devon

Visit our website at www.davidandcharles.co.uk

David & Charles books are available from all good
bookshops; alternatively you can contact our Orderline on
(0)1626 334555 or write to us at FREEPOST EX2 110,
David & Charles Direct, Newton Abbot TQ12 4ZZ, UK
(no stamp required UK mainland).

CONTENTS

INTRODUCTION

his book is inspired by the fine textile works created in England in the 16th century, the reign of the Tudor kings and queens and especially Queen Elizabeth, and in the 17th century under their Stuart successors. This was also the time when the Renaissance style reached Britain and influenced court circles in architecture, art, music, poetry and literature. In England it was a period of some stability after the Wars of the Roses, with a strong monarchy and an atmosphere of confidence and increasing wealth. Enormous numbers of houses were built and had to be furnished, and as furniture was simple and un-upholstered it needed cushions, while the draughty walls needed tapestries and hangings. Women decorated household goods and clothing and in their hands embroidery became enormously inventive and self confident. At a time when printing had only just been invented and was rare, all fabrics were plain except for the expensive, finely woven imported damasks.

Society at this time was increasingly secular and no longer was all fine embroidery made for the Church. Portraits of the time show many embroidered pieces, most of which have not survived. Some clothes have embroidery all over – on sleeves, bodices and skirts. There was a clear delight in brightly coloured silks, which can still be appreciated in some treasured museum examples and in portrait details. Many housewives produced yards of lace for ruffs and cuffs. Beds, too, offered lots of scope for embroidery: pillowcases embroidered all over in blackwork, canvaswork (needlepoint) valances and appliquéd bed curtains all give an idea of the richness of decoration.

Some lovely 'slips' survive, small pieces of embroidery that were used to decorate large projects such as bed curtains. They usually consisted of flowers, birds or animals and were stitched in silk on fine canvas using tent stitch. The flowers were often beautifully coloured and naturalistic, resembling those used in the early herbals.

The finished pieces were cut round then applied to a larger piece of fabric by oversewing round the edge, sometimes with a metallic thread. One advantage was that these slips could be applied to velvet for rich cushions.

During this period flowers were treasured and gardens were inventively developed into clever arrangements of growing 'knots' in imitation of Renaissance examples from France and Italy. My collection of boxes on pages 48–54 features knots, all based on the structure of 16th-century examples but embroidered in different styles. One uses the favourite heart motif, another combines beads with cross stitch and another fills the 'beds' with blackwork patterns, which were extremely popular in Tudor times.

The foliate flourishes of Renaissance style also provided the inspiration for the elegant table linen on page 22.

Designs in the heartsease collection (page 6) also reflect the interest in gardens. The notebook is copied from one stitched by Princess Elizabeth as a girl but is obviously influenced by the knot garden. Very beautiful embroidered book covers survive from the 16th century. They are luxurious pieces, often worked on red velvet using metallic threads to enhance the valuable and still-rare printed texts. Some incorporated pearls and gems and had gold clasps. Small, rectangular embroidered cushions survive: these are thought to have been made to lay a book upon whilst reading, to protect the fine cover. A precious book in an embroidered binding would have been a suitable gift for a King or Queen. Gloves were desirable presents as well, with the gauntlets covered in embroidery.

I particularly enjoy the inventiveness of the many Elizabethan textiles covered in scrolling, all-over patterns that include flowers and insects. The originals are quite small and were worked in a wide variety of fine embroidery stitches. These often included three-dimensional details for insect wings or opening pea-pods. It was a pleasure to select details and translate them into the coiling cross stitch pictures on page 56.

I also enjoyed creating the drawstring bags on pages 76–80, based on gifts to Queen Elizabeth I. The originals were much smaller and the materials more costly, including real gold and silver metallic threads, gems and pearls. I have included 'pearls' and beads as the original embroiderers did. The black bag with its all-over pattern in metallic thread and bright gillyflowers is an example of the sort of design used for a variety of embroidered pieces, including cushions, stool covers and bags. These all-over designs were always disciplined: motifs did not flow over the surface but were contained in a geometrical network. Several other examples taken from costume detail, samplers and pattern books have been included in the Motif Library beginning on page 85.

My bell pull and cushion designs on pages 12–14 are filled with colourful fruits and flowers and are based on tapestries produced by the Sheldon looms, established in the 1560s. In the inspirational tapestry, the fruits, flowers, animals and birds are interspersed with classical figures epitomizing virtues. The borders are crammed with fruit and flowers and little scenes of everyday life in the country. With a tapestry like that on your wall you would continually find delightful new discoveries in the feast of colourful details.

Elizabethans requiring embroidered hangings for their walls or embroidered carpets for their tables frequently employed professional embroiderers, usually men, who often travelled about the country from one employer to another. They would sometimes draw out designs on canvas for ladies to embroider. Another way to transfer designs to fabric was to borrow a page from one of the new books published for embroiderers and lacemakers. By pricking around the outlines and pouncing chalk through the holes, a design could be transferred to canvas. Women collected and stored examples of attractive designs on their samplers.

My sampler design on page 26 is typical of the time when samplers began to be used to teach young girls a repertoire of stitches and patterns, when a long, narrow format allowed lots of different bands to be included. They would have been used for working cushions, for borders on domestic linens, for decorating seams on clothing, for collars and ruffs, for marking linen, and sometimes recorded the name and age of the stitcher. I've tried to retain the typical features and bright colours of the originals whilst keeping to cross stitch and straight stitches.

In many ways the embroidery of the early 17th century was indistinguishable from that of the preceding century, but there were some new departures. It was a time when

the education of young girls became more organized. They progressed from learning to sew samplers to embroidering decorated boxes or caskets and pictures, usually showing Biblical stories. These pictures included countryside scenes, trees, flowers, animals and insects. Groups of figures stand amongst dogs, deer, lions, leopards, elephants, camels, frogs and birds. The bountiful tree firescreen on page 64 is based on a work of this time (which explains the camel and parrot!), reflecting too this exciting time of world exploration, of trading links with the East Indies and the early settlement of America.

The embroidery of the Elizabethan period is characterized by great richness and originality. The works are often more complex than modern ones, often on a finer scale and frequently allude to historical figures, but in them we recognize the beginning of all the embroidery we know today. I hope you are inspired, as I was, by such beautiful pieces of work.

HEARTSEASE
COLLECTION

Yet mark'd I where the bolt of Cupid fell.
It fell upon a little western flower,
Before milk-white, now purple with love's wound,
And maidens call it Love-in-idleness.

(From William Shakespeare's *A Midsummer-Night's Dream*, Act II, Scene i)

The heartsease or wild pansy was one of the wild flowers that Tudor gardeners adopted as a garden plant. It became a favourite for needlework as well and nearly every early sampler had a heartsease motif somewhere. It was one of the favourite flowers of Queen Elizabeth I: she wore them on her costume in at least two portraits and had them

embroidered in blackwork on her clothes. As a young princess she made an embroidered cover for a book she wrote by hand as a present for her stepmother, Katherine Parr. This book still exists in the Bodleian Library in Oxford, England. It features four heartsease flowers around a geometric interlaced pattern and it inspired the notebook cover design in this section.

The plant has been given a wide variety of common names over the centuries: Herb Trinity and Three Faces in a Hood, suggested by its appearance and colouring; Love in Idleness, Tickle Me Fancy and Call Me to You, reflecting its potency in love charms. In *A Midsummer-Night's Dream* it is rubbed on Titania's eyes so that she falls in love with the first creature she sees on waking.

The heartsease motif lends itself well to cross stitch designs and I have used it to decorate a notebook cover, a bowl lid and a card. The heartsease on the card comes from a 17th-century sampler, while the bowl lid design combines stitching with 'jewels', as was the fashion in the dress worn in the Tudor court.

The heartsease, or wild pansy flower, creates a colourful display in three designs, perfect for decorating a card, bowl lid and book cover.

Heartsease Notebook Cover

STITCH COUNT
101 x 71
DESIGN SIZE
18.5 x 13cm (7¼ x 5in) approx

MATERIALS
63 x 32cm (25 x 12½in)
14-count navy blue Aida
•
Tapestry needle size 26
•
Stranded cotton (floss) as listed
•
Kreinik Fine (#8) Braid as listed
•
A5 [21 x 15cm (8¾ x 6in)] notebook
•
33 x 21.5cm (13 x 8½in)
fusible interfacing

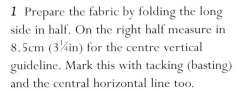

1 Prepare the fabric by folding the long side in half. On the right half measure in 8.5cm (3¼in) for the centre vertical guideline. Mark this with tacking (basting) and the central horizontal line too.

2 Follow the chart, working over one block of Aida and using two strands of stranded cotton (floss) throughout and single lengths of fine braid. Begin with the lilac cross and gold square, then the outer border using the braid. Work the inner border using stranded cotton (floss). Embroider the lilac interlaced patterns around the metallic lines.

3 Work the flowers using two strands for cross stitch and backstitch. The green lines can be worked by making stitches that pass through the fabric two blocks from where they start, which is less likely to get caught than very long stitches. Work the purple lines as single long stitches. When the embroidery is complete remove guidelines and press (see page 97).

4 This project used an A5 notebook as listed but making up will depend on the size of your chosen notebook – see page 100.

STRANDED COTTONS

COLOUR	DMC	ANCHOR	MADEIRA	SKEINS
Lilac	553	98	0712	1
Light lilac	554	96	0711	1
Dark lilac	550	102	0714	1
Lemon	445	288	0103	1
Yellow	973	290	0105	1
Orange	742	303	0107	1
Green	702	226	1306	1

KREINIK FINE (#8) BRAID

COLOUR		REELS
Light gold	102HL	2
Lilac	023	1

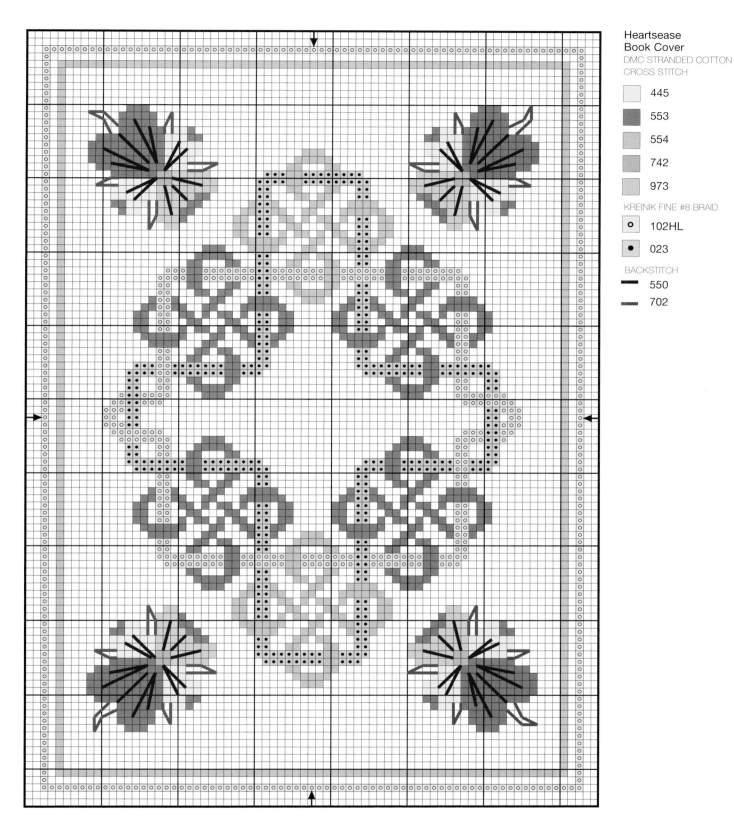

Heartsease
Book Cover
DMC STRANDED COTTON
CROSS STITCH

	445
	553
	554
	742
	973

KREINIK FINE #8 BRAID

◉	102HL
●	023

BACKSTITCH

━━	550
━━	702

*You could stitch just the central pattern of interlaced lines to
create a stylish card. The colours could also be changed – try
copper and mauves, silver and greens or gold and blues.*

Wild Pansy Bowl

STITCH COUNT
41 x 41
DESIGN SIZE
5.8cm (2¼in) diameter approx

MATERIALS
15 x 15cm (6 x 6in)
18-count navy blue Aida *or*
18 x 18cm (7 x 7in) 14-count Aida
•
Tapestry needle size 26 and
a beading needle
•
Stranded cotton (floss) as listed
•
Mill Hill seed beads,
four pearl and one mauve
•
9 x 9cm (3½ x 3½in)
fusible interfacing
•
Blue medium ceramic bowl
(Framecraft code PL3 *or*
if on 14-count Aida use 8.9cm (3½in)
bowl code PL5, see Suppliers)

1 Prepare the fabric and mark the centre lines with tacking (basting) (see page 97).

2 Follow the chart, working over one block of Aida and beginning in the centre. Use one strand of stranded cotton (floss) for cross stitch and backstitch on 18-count fabric or two strands on 14-count.

3 Attach four pearl or cream beads (also used for some of the bags on pages 76 and 80) and one mauve bead, using matching thread and a beading needle.

4 When the embroidery is complete remove guidelines and press (see page 97). Iron interfacing on to the back and using the template provided with the bowl, cut out a circle to fit in the lid, and then assemble according to the manufacturer's instructions.

You could replace the pearl and mauve beads with beads or metallic thread in other colours – try gold, yellow, orange or green.

STRANDED COTTONS

COLOUR	DMC	ANCHOR	MADEIRA	SKEINS
Cream	746	386	0101	1
Yellow	973	290	0105	1
Dark green	367	210	1312	1
Green	368	214	1310	1
Violet	210	108	0802	1
Dark violet	3837	99	2709	1
Orange	742	314	0201	1

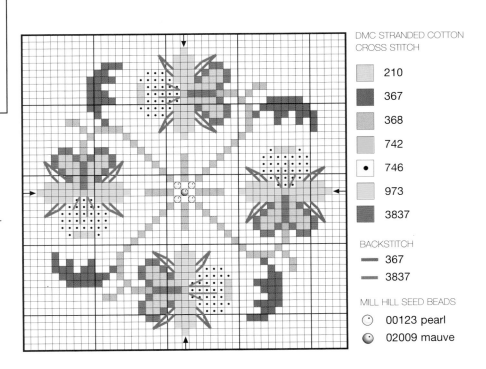

DMC STRANDED COTTON CROSS STITCH

▨	210
▨	367
▨	368
▨	742
•	746
▨	973
▨	3837

BACKSTITCH
— 367
— 3837

MILL HILL SEED BEADS
☉ 00123 pearl
◉ 02009 mauve

Pansy and Bee Card

STITCH COUNT
40 x 38
DESIGN SIZE
7.25 x 7cm (2⅞ x 2¾in) approx

MATERIALS
6 x 4in (15 x 10cm) 14-count cream
Aida (Zweigart code 264)
or 28 count cream evenweave

•

Tapestry needle size 26

•

Stranded cotton (floss) as listed

•

Violet greetings card with
8cm (3¼in) aperture

•

15 x 10cm (6 x 4in) fusible interfacing

•

Double-sided adhesive tape

1 Prepare the fabric and mark the centre lines with tacking (basting) (see page 97).

2 Follow the chart, beginning in the centre and working over one block of Aida or two evenweave threads. Use two strands of stranded cotton (floss) to cross stitch the heartsease and the bee's body but only one strand of DMC 3802 for the wings. Use one strand for backstitches.

3 When the embroidery is complete remove guidelines and press (see page 97). Mount into a card using interfacing and double-sided tape (see page 99).

This design would make an attractive picture framed with a simple cross-stitched border in matching shades.

STRANDED COTTONS

COLOUR	DMC	ANCHOR	MADEIRA	SKEINS
Light violet	210	108	0802	1
Mid violet	208	111	0804	1
Dark violet	550	102	0714	1
Cream	746	386	0101	1
Lemon	445	288	0103	1
Yellow	973	290	0105	1
Orange	972	298	0107	1
Green	368	214	1310	1
Dark green	367	210	1312	1
Dark antique mauve	3802	1019	0601	1

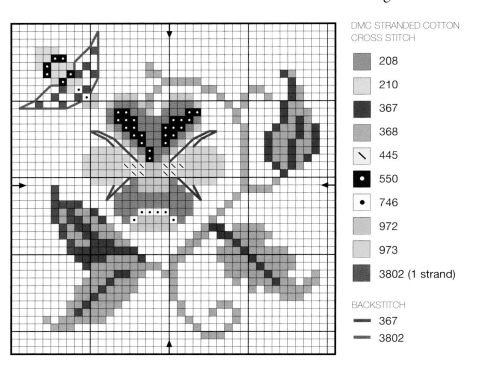

DMC STRANDED COTTON
CROSS STITCH

▨	208
▢	210
▨	367
▨	368
＼	445
●	550
•	746
▨	972
▨	973
■	3802 (1 strand)

BACKSTITCH
— 367
— 3802

SHELDON TAPESTRY INSPIRATION

Feed him with apricots and dewberries,
With purple grapes, green figs and mulberries;

(From William Shakespeare's *A Midsummer-Night's Dream*, Act III, Scene i)

In Tudor times, tapestries provided warmth and comfort as well as colour and pattern. They were essential items for noble and aspiring families, who would take their tapestries, cushions and bed hangings when they moved from one house to another. Most were expensive items imported from Flanders.

In 1561, William Sheldon founded a successful tapestry factory in Warwickshire to provide an alternative to the Flemish imports. His family were in the wool business and England was producing the finest quality wool at that time. He sent one of his men to Flanders to learn the tapestry technique and he returned with equipment and Flemish weavers. Designs on William Sheldon's early tapestries were Old Testament stories, later ones included maps or mythological scenes. The tapestry that inspired my embroideries includes a framed biblical scene, set into a background crammed with country flowers, birds and animals. The biblical figures are no bigger than the pheasants, heron or unicorn featured amongst the flowers of the background.

Tapestry borders are often a great source for designs and the borders of Sheldon tapestries are no exception.

The borders have a red background, which makes the fruits and flowers look rich and inviting, so I used the same colour fabric for my designs. Vases filled with glorious flowers and overflowing with fruits and vegetables provided the inspiration for my tapestry-style bell pull and cushion. The cushion uses some of the extra borders from the tapestry to surround the fruit and flowers.

I designed the cushion as a square to be more in keeping with our needs today but in the Elizabethan period, long rectangular cushions were often embroidered to soften wooden benches and stone window seats.

The bell pull features a Renaissance-style vase filled with roses, foliage of all sorts, and berries. It is being visited by birds, and near the top has a collection of apples, pears, melon and other fruits. The square cushion has grapes, pomegranate, plum and apple. The attractive borders that frame the central motif could be reused for another design of your choice – refer to the Motif Library beginning on page 85, which contains a number of suitable designs.

The bell pull and cushion, inspired by the 1611 Sheldon tapestries, are a delight to stitch, worked in whole cross stitch in a warm and welcoming palette of colours. If you prefer, the cushion design would also make an attractive top for a footstool.

Sheldon Bell Pull and Cushion

STITCH COUNTS
Bell Pull 347 x 68
Cushion 169 x 169

DESIGN SIZES
Bell Pull 63.5 x 12.5cm (25 x 5in)
Cushion 30 x 30cm (12 x 12in)

MATERIALS
Stranded cotton (floss) as listed

•

Tapestry needle size 26

For the Bell Pull
86 x 26cm (34 x 10in) 14-count
Victorian red Aida
(Fabric Flair N14.969)

•

64 x 15cm (25 x 6in) backing fabric
and stiff interfacing

•

2m (2¼yd) braid for edging

•

Tassel (optional)

•

15cm (6in) wide bell-pull ends
(Viking Loom, design G, MWP03)

For the Cushion
43 x 43cm (17 x 17in) 14-count
Victorian red Aida
(Fabric Flair N14.969)

•

38 x 38cm (15 x 15in) backing fabric

•

30 x 30cm (12 x 12in) cushion pad

•

1.5m (1½yd) braid to trim

TO WORK THE BELL PULL
1 Prepare the fabric and mark the centre lines with tacking (basting) (see page 97). Mark further guidelines 90 blocks above and below the centre.

2 Work from the centre of the fabric and the centre of the chart on pages 15–17 over one block of Aida. Use two strands of stranded cotton (floss) for cross stitch, checking your position frequently.

3 When the embroidery is complete, remove guidelines, press (see page 97) and make up into a bell pull (page 100).

TO WORK THE CUSHION
1 Prepare the fabric and mark the centre lines with tacking (basting) (see page 97).

2 Work from the centre of the fabric and the centre of the chart on pages 18–21 over one block of Aida. Use two strands of stranded cotton (floss) for cross stitch. You might find it useful to have two needles threaded with different colours.

3 When the embroidery is complete, remove guidelines and press (see page 97). Make up as a cushion cover as described on page 101.

CUSHION STRANDED COTTONS

COLOUR	DMC	ANCHOR	MADEIRA	SKEINS
Pale blue green	3816	876	1207	1
Blue green	501	877	1704	2
Very dark blue green	500	879	1705	1
Green light	470	266	1410	1
Green med	469	267	1608	1
Green dark	936	263	1508	1
Light straw	3821	891	2208	2
Old gold lt	833	874	2203	1
Gold	783	307	2211	2
Old gold dk	831	855	2201	1
Tan medium	436	1045	2011	1
Dark brown	838	381	2003	2
Light orange	742	303	0107	1
Red copper	918	351	0314	1
Red	817	46	0211	1
Toffee	780	365	2214	1
Beige grey	822	926	1908	1
Yellow beige	3046	887	2206	1

Bell Pull
DMC STRANDED COTTON
CROSS STITCH

—	420	■	902
I	436	■	918
■	469	×	922
■	470	⊙	936
■	472		3046
/	500		3816
■	501	+	3821
○	720	/	3852
T	742	•	3865
■	782		
■	817		
\	822		

BELL PULL STRANDED COTTONS

COLOUR	DMC	ANCHOR	MADEIRA	SKEINS
Pale blue green	3816	876	1207	1
Very dark blue green	501	877	1704	1
Blue green	500	879	1705	2
Very pale green	472	264	1414	1
Light green	470	266	1410	1
Medium green	469	267	1608	2
Dark green	936	263	1508	2
Light straw	3821	891	2208	1
Dark straw	3852	306	2209	1
Dark gold	782	901	2212	1
Dark copper	918	351	0314	1
Flowerpot	922	1003	0311	1
Dark garnet	902	897	1608	1
Red	817	46	0211	1
Light orange	742	303	0107	1
Dark orange	720	326	0309	1
Yellow beige	3046	887	2206	1
Beige grey	822	926	1908	1
Hazelnut	420	375	2105	1
Medium tan	436	1045	2011	1
Winter white	3865	2	white	1

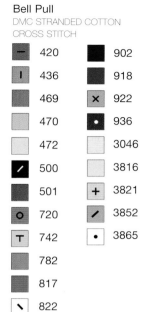

Bell Pull
DMC STRANDED COTTON
CROSS STITCH

—	420	■	902
I	436	■	918
	469	×	922
	470	⊙	936
	472		3046
/	500		3816
	501	+	3821
⊙	720	/	3852
T	742	•	3865
	782		
	817		
\	822		

Cushion

DMC STRANDED COTTON
CROSS STITCH

I	436		831
	469		833
	470		838
/	500		918
	501	•	936
△	780	+	972
L	783		3046
	817		3816
\	822		3821

Cushion

DMC STRANDED COTTON
CROSS STITCH

I	436		831
	469		833
	470		838
/	500	●	936
	501	+	972
△	780		3046
L	783		3816
	817		3821
\	822		

RENAISSANCE TABLE LINEN

How to Bake Orenges
Faire peele your Orenges and pick away all the white that is
under the peele, and so lay them in a fine paste, and put into
them sugar, very little Sinamon or none at all, but a little
Ginger and bake them leisurely.

(From *A Book of Cookrye* A.W. London 1591)

These elegant Renaissance designs were inspired by the painted wooden wall panelling at Hardwick Hall in Derbyshire, England, one of the great Elizabethan houses. They lend themselves particularly well to the square design of a coaster, so to elongate the design for the table mat I looked at similar designs for embroidery, cutwork and lace-making in *A Schole-house for the Needle* printed in 1632. This has pages of border patterns, one of which has been used for the mat design. The foliate flourishes used in the pattern book perfectly matched the Hardwick Hall decorations. The interlaced design in the centre, taken from the pattern book, is typically 16th century.

The Renaissance style was an international one and would have been very familiar to Bess of Hardwick. She was an ambitious and powerful woman who was responsible for several great houses during her lifetime. Renaissance design and ornamentation were important during the time she was married to the Earl of Shrewsbury. He was ordered by Queen Elizabeth to accommodate Mary, Queen of Scots, though Mary was, in fact, a prisoner. Needlework was allowed by Elizabeth, even encouraged by the supply of materials, and fortunately Bess shared Mary's interest in it. The two women spent their days devising works and embroidering together. The Renaissance style remained popular in decoration for some centuries and retains its charm today.

These designs can be adapted to suit any décor by choosing a different colour of Aida and threads – perhaps a pale fabric with darker cottons. Alternatively, black with gold embroidery would be magnificent.

22

Renaissance Table Mat and Coasters

TABLE MAT STITCH COUNT
177 x 50
DESIGN SIZE
32 x 9.5cm (12½ x 3½in) approx
FINISHED MAT SIZE
40 x 32cm (15½ x 12½in) approx

MATERIALS
46 x 40cm (16 x 18in)
14-count colonel blue Aida
(Zweigart code 522)
•
Tapestry needle size 26
•
Stranded cotton (floss) as listed

TABLE MAT STRANDED COTTONS

COLOUR	DMC	ANCHOR	MADEIRA	SKEINS
Dark blue	820	134	0904	1
Mid blue	825	162	1011	1
Gold	783	307	2211	1
Dark gold	780	365	2214	1

Allow one skein each of dark blue and gold for each mat, and half a skein of mid blue. One skein of the dark gold will be more than enough for a set of four mats.

TO WORK A TABLE MAT

1 Fold the fabric in half both ways. The stitching is to be on the right-hand edge. Measure 15cm (6in) from the centre fold and use tacking (basting) stitches to mark a vertical guideline in the centre of the area to be stitched. Mark the horizontal guideline in the stitching area.

2 Follow the chart, working over one block of Aida. Start cross stitching with two strands at the centre using the gold, changing to dark blue as you move out. Work backstitch using one strand.

3 When the embroidery is complete, remove guidelines and press (see page 97). The edges of the mat can be hemmed or fringed. Trim to the size required for your chosen edging. To create a fringe, machine stitch round the edges using matching sewing thread, then withdraw the Aida threads from the edge to the machine-stitched line.

TO WORK A COASTER

1 Prepare the fabric, marking centre lines with tacking (basting). Stitch over one Aida block, working from the centre of the fabric and chart. Use two strands of stranded cotton (floss) for cross stitch and one for backstitch.

2 When the embroidery is complete, remove guidelines and press. Trim the fabric according to the finish required. If using a coaster, iron interfacing to the back of the fabric, trim to the coaster template size and assemble. Alternatively, create a fringe as in step 3, above.

COASTERS STITCH COUNTS
Large 48 x 48
Small 38 x 38
DESIGN SIZES
Large 9 x 9cm (3½ x 3½in)
Small 6.5 x 6.5cm (2¾ x 2¾in)

MATERIALS
8 x 8in (20 x 20cm)
14-count colonel blue Aida
(Zweigart code 522)
•
Tapestry needle size 26
•
Stranded cotton (floss) as listed
•
Optional square plastic coaster to fit design (from Fabric Flair, see Suppliers)
•
Optional fusible interfacing

COASTERS STRANDED COTTONS

COLOUR	DMC	ANCHOR	MADEIRA	SKEINS
Dark blue	820	134	0904	1
Mid blue	825	162	1011	1
Gold	783	307	2211	1

These amounts are sufficient for two large coasters or four small.

Coasters

DMC STRANDED COTTON
CROSS STITCH

	780
	783
	820
	825

BACKSTITCH

— 783

— 820

Table Mat

BAND SAMPLER PATTERNS

We, Hermia . . . have with our needles created both one flower,
Both on one sampler, sitting on one cushion.

(From William Shakespeare's *A Midsummer-Night's Dream*, Act III, Scene ii)

Samplers, which can be compared to stitched notebooks, began as examples of embroidery patterns in the years before printed material was available. These samplers contained enough of a border pattern to work from, details of all-over patterns and examples of flowers, birds or animals. They included examples of different stitches as well as designs, and in an age when lace was fashionable, 'lace' patterns that could be created by needlework.

No one can say exactly when samplers began to be made but writers in the 16th century were certainly familiar with them. From 1502 a record exists of a length of linen 'for a sampler for the Queen'. Shakespeare wrote of two friends, who as young girls had worked together on a single flower in a sampler. Another playwright described how a lady would study her sampler before deciding which style of work would be most suitable for a ruff, collar, sleeve, hood or cap, and which lace to edge it with and which stitch to use. Samplers were a valuable pattern resource, treasured in the workbox. They became family assets, bequeathed from one generation to the next.

The earliest dated sampler survives from the end of the 16th century, and a considerable number still exist from the 17th century. It was during this century that the sampler began to change from a lady's collection of useful patterns, collected as she would recipes, to an exercise for young girls learning to embroider. By this time printed pattern books were becoming available and they began to fulfil the function for which the working sampler had been so necessary. It was the time when the long, narrow band sampler format developed, each band containing a different pattern, border or technique, stretching from side to side of the linen fabric. As well as coloured patterns and sometimes blackwork patterns worked in silks, they often included whitework bands worked in linen thread. These might include satin stitch, cutwork, where an area of the fabric was cut out and then filled with needlelace patterns, and drawn work, where threads were drawn and stitched together. Towards the end of the century they began to include the embroiderer's name and age or date, and sometimes the name of her teacher.

My band sampler has been left in an unframed state, finished with rods at the top and bottom in memory of old samplers that were rolled on to rods and stored in workboxes. This one, whilst still accessible and touchable, can be suspended.

This band sampler creates a wonderful focal point and is straightforward to stitch. If you prefer, you could use the alphabet to stitch your name, age and date. The banded patterns within the sampler can also be used to create all sorts of other smaller projects, such as the carnation bag and little sampler mat shown on pages 30 and 31.

Band Sampler

1 Prepare the fabric and mark the centre of the long axis with tacking (basting) (see page 97). As the design is a long one it might help to mount the fabric in an embroidery frame.

2 Use two strands of stranded cotton (floss) and work over two threads of evenweave for all the cross stitch and backstitch. For the whitework section, use one and two strands of white as indicated on the chart (see picture opposite), working satin stitch lines the lengths indicated on the chart and over one fabric thread in width. Note, the satin stitches are shown in dark grey on the chart for clarity.

3 With reference to the layout opposite, work the various bands as follows:
Band 1 Start with the top carnation band on the chart on page 32, about 7.5cm (3in) down from the top of the fabric, in cross stitch and backstitch.

Band 2 Work the two blackwork patterns using backstitch.
Band 3 Work the whitework section in long straight stitches (see satin stitch, page 98), using one strand of white for the thin lines on the chart and two strands for the thicker lines. Using a magnifying glass will help.
Band 4 Change to two strands of cotton (floss) and work two blackwork patterns over two fabric threads in backstitch.
Bands 5, 6, 7, 8 and 9 Work the three floral patterns and the alphabet and finish with the spot motifs at the bottom of the chart in cross stitch and backstitch.

4 When the embroidery is complete, check for missed stitches, remove the guidelines and press (see page 97). Hem the long edges or fold in and press before fusing interfacing to the back. Wrap the top and bottom edges over the bell pull ends, slipstitching in place at the back of the embroidery.

STRANDED COTTONS

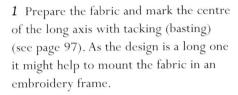

COLOUR	DMC	ANCHOR	MADEIRA	SKEINS
White	blanc	1	white	1
Blue	517	169	1107	1
Misty blue	807	168	1109	1
Dark green	904	258	1413	1
Green	470	266	1410	1
Rose pink	335	38	0610	1
Pale pink	962	75	0609	1
Red	321	47	0510	1
Orange	900	332	0208	1
Yellow	725	305	0106	1
Brown	839	1050	1913	1

Many parts of the sampler could be used for a range of smaller projects. For example, any of the blackwork or floral bands would make lovely adornments for towels or bed linen if stitched on Aida or linen band.
See pages 30–31 for further ideas.

Band 1 This is a very popular carnation border that many embroiderers copied on to their samplers. To use it as a continuous border the green parallel lines are continued to the level of the top of the pattern and the design 'flipped'. The carnation bag overleaf uses an adapted version of this part of the design.

Band 2 Two bands of blackwork: good practice for the blackwork used extensively in 16th and 17th century clothes and linen.

Band 3 The whitework section has six satin-stitched designs achieved by straight stitches worked closely together.

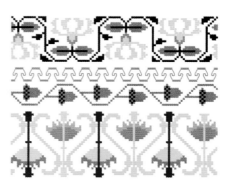

If you prefer to work over two evenweave threads or one block of Aida, you could substitute patterns from page 95 of the Motif Library for the whitework section.

Band 4 Two different, slightly deeper blackwork patterns worked in backstitch. Alternatively, you could use double running stitch (see page 98).

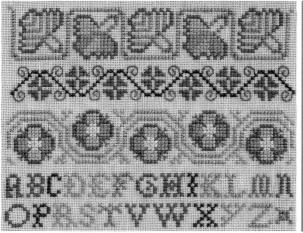

Bands 5, 6, 7 and 8 This section features three floral bands and an alphabet. The letter forms have been copied from 17th-century examples, where letters J and Q were omitted because they were very similar to other letters. U and W were sometimes stitched by inverting N and M.

Band 9 This bottom band contains a collection of typical spot motifs – carnation, swan, fruit tree, tulip and butterfly. They could be used to decorate a variety of small items, for example, the tulip is stitched in the centre of a little sampler mat on page 31.

Carnation Bag

STITCH COUNT
54 x 82

DESIGN SIZE
10 x 15cm (4 x 6in) approx

MATERIALS
26 x 43cm (10 x 17in) navy blue
14-count Aida
(Zweigart code 589)

•

Tapestry needle size 26

•

Stranded cotton (floss) as listed

•

Metallic thread as listed

•

20 x 36cm (8 x 14in) lining fabric in
blue or contrasting colour

•

Matching sewing thread

•

1m (1yd) black cord or ribbon

1 The design is worked on the bottom third of the length of Aida to make the flap of an 'envelope' bag. Work a tacking (basting) guideline in sewing thread 10cm (4in) up from the bottom and a vertical line halfway across the fabric.

2 Use two strands of stranded cotton (floss) for cross stitch and backstitch, and two strands of metallic thread for the centre knot. You could substitute any suitable fragment of metallic thread or use a pale stranded cotton to give a good contrast. When the embroidery is complete remove the guidelines and press before making up the bag.

3 Trim the embroidered fabric to the same size as the lining fabric piece. Pin the pieces right sides together and stitch around all edges, two blocks outside the green border all round, leaving a gap for turning. Trim off excess fabric, turn to the right side and stitch the gap. Press the embroidery from the back, using towelling underneath to avoid flattening the stitches. Fold the bottom third of the lined fabric up and slipstitch the sides together. The top third now forms the embroidered flap of the bag. Attach the ribbon or cord strap, stitching it to the inside of the bag.

This bright design has been reworked from the main sampler. It has only small changes from the top pattern of the band sampler, the dark blue background giving a distinctive look. Different greens complement the fabric but you could choose your own. As your hands stitch, allow your mind to dwell on the young women of 400 years ago as they stitched the same pattern.

STRANDED COTTONS

COLOUR	DMC	ANCHOR	MADEIRA	SKEINS
Misty blue	807	168	1109	1
Dark emerald	910	229	1302	1
Light emerald	912	205	1213	1
Rose pink	335	38	0610	1
Red	321	47	0510	1

STRANDED METALLIC

COLOUR	DMC
Metallic pink	5288

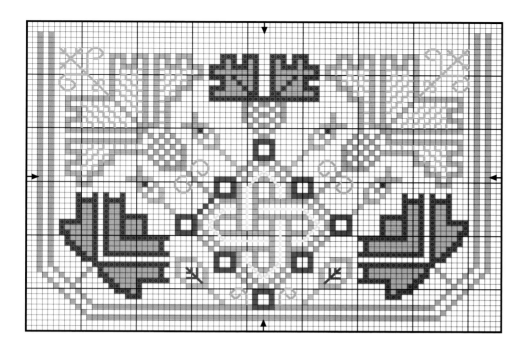

The central interlaced knot could be stitched for a matching key ring.

DMC STRANDED COTTON
CROSS STITCH

⊙	321
	335
	807
	910
	912

BACKSTITCH
▬	335
▬	807
▬	912
	5288 metallic

This little mat is an adaptation of band 6 of the sampler charted on page 33, framing a tulip motif from band 9. The design has been cross stitched over two threads on a 15 x 15cm (6 x 6in) piece of antique white 27-count Linda. To create a fringe, use matching sewing thread to machine stitch a line about 1cm (½in) from the design all round, then withdraw the fabric threads up to the line.

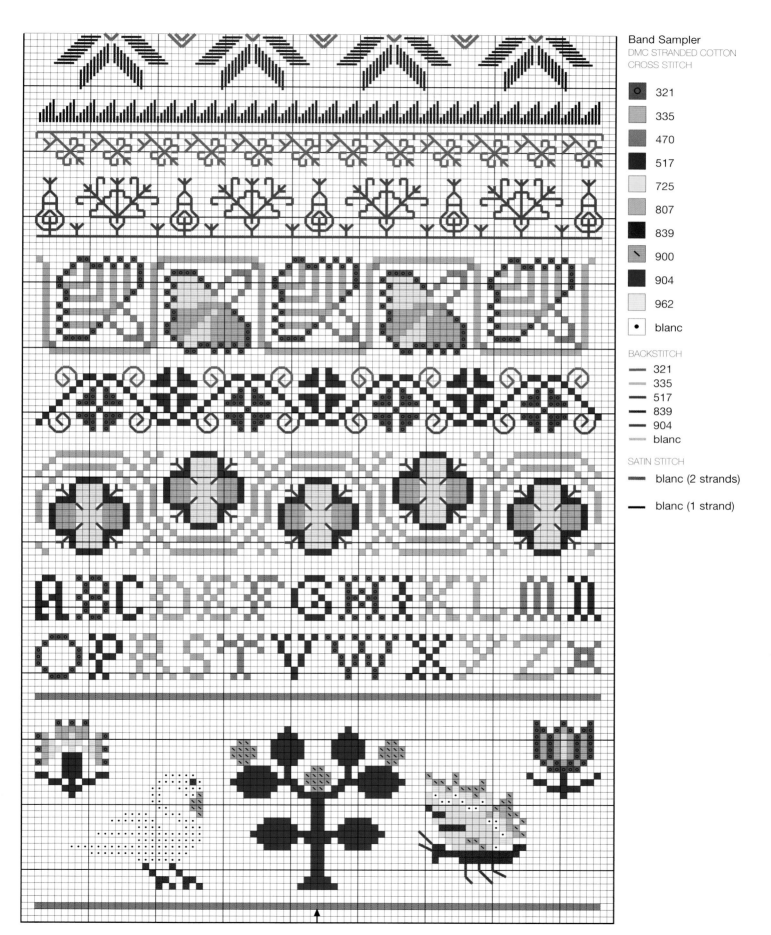

Band Sampler
DMC STRANDED COTTON
CROSS STITCH

○	321
	335
	470
	517
	725
	807
	839
╲	900
	904
	962
•	blanc

BACKSTITCH

—	321
—	335
—	517
—	839
—	904
—	blanc

SATIN STITCH

▬	blanc (2 strands)
—	blanc (1 strand)

FOUR SEASONS FLORALS

. . . a good heart's worth gold.

(From William Shakespeare's *King Henry IV*, Part II, Act II, Scene ii)

Thus lovely flower designs are based on a beautiful cushion embroidered in London around 1600 (now in the Victoria and Albert Museum, London). The cushion cover is a square of red satin covered in a network of hearts, arranged like the ones in the background pattern. Designs of this period frequently had an all-over network with other details added at intervals.

In the original embroidery, the twenty-one hearts that made up the design each contained a different flower, symmetrically arranged and stylized to fit the heart shape. All the plants spring from the same point in the heart and the lines of stems and leaves make graceful curves which are a continuation of the outline of the heart. The embroidery used gold and silver threads, metal strips and coloured silks and was edged with metallic lace.

The Elizabethan designer clearly wished to show off the red satin fabric, enhancing it but not obscuring it with the skilful embroidery. My designs also use the fabric as an important element, with gold-flecked Aida selected to give the designs the all-over glitter of the original embroidery.

The plants chosen to represent the seasons are the bluebell for spring, marigold for summer, acorn for autumn and holly for winter.

These attractive designs look wonderful as a set of cushions and would be eye-catching in any room of the house.

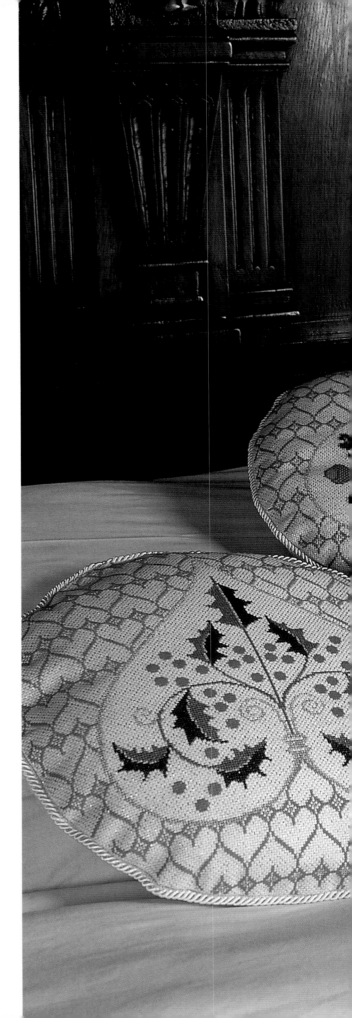

Four Seasons Cushions

FOR EACH CUSHION

STITCH COUNTS
209 x 209
DESIGN SIZES
38 x 38cm (15 x 15in) approx

MATERIALS
50 x 50cm (20 x 20in)
14-count gold-flecked Aida
(Zweigart code 118)

•

Tapestry needle size 26

•

Stranded cotton (floss) and metallic
gold thread as listed

•

46 x 46cm (18 x 18in) backing fabric

•

38cm (16in) diameter cushion pad

•

130cm (50in) length of braid
or metallic gold lace

TO WORK EACH DESIGN

1 Prepare the fabric and mark the centre lines with tacking (basting) (see page 97). If stitching several cushions, arrange the Aida fabric so the direction of the gold fleck is consistent.

2 Following the chart of your choice (see pages 38–45), begin cross stitching the central heart with gold thread. Use this thread as it comes from the reel (see page 96 for advice on using metallic thread). Using two strands of stranded cotton (floss) work the background pattern of hearts. Complete the pattern by working the gold details. Embroider the plant details, leaving until last the gold thread outline around the leaves, the curls on the acorn and the leaf ribs and curls on the holly.

3 When the embroidery is complete, remove guidelines and press (see page 97). Refer to page 101 for making up into a cushion.

Spring

In this cushion, the bluebell represents spring, as bluebell woods are so lovely in the spring before the trees come into leaf.

SPRING BLUEBELL STRANDED COTTONS

COLOUR	DMC	ANCHOR	MADEIRA	SKEINS
Light blue	813	161	1013	3
Mid blue	798	137	0911	1
Dark blue	803	148	1010	1
Green	561	212	1205	1

COATS OPHIR GOLD THREAD		REELS
Gold	300	1

Summer

Summer is represented by the
marigold, as this bright flower is
so sunlike in both shape and colour.

SUMMER MARIGOLD
STRANDED COTTONS

COLOUR	DMC	ANCHOR	MADEIRA	SKEINS
Pale orange	3854	323	2514	3
Rust	900	332	0208	1
Orange	740	316	0202	1
Petal gold	741	314	0201	1
Yellow	742	303	0107	1
Brown	400	351	2305	1
Green	905	257	1412	1

COATS OPHIR GOLD THREAD		REELS
Gold	300	1

This set of four designs would make a
charming and unusual display of
pictures if framed in circular mounts,
then hung in a hallway or
dining room, for example.

Autumn

The acorn represents autumn,
when the nuts ripen. They were favourite
motifs in Elizabethan times, perhaps
because oaks were so important for the
building of houses and ships.

AUTUMN ACORN
STRANDED COTTONS

COLOUR	DMC	ANCHOR	MADEIRA	SKEINS
Old gold	832	907	2202	3
Nut	436	1045	2011	1
Nutty brown	780	365	2214	1
Antique gold	831	855	2201	1
Green	904	258	1413	1

COATS OPHIR GOLD THREAD		REELS
Gold	300	1

Winter

Winter is represented by the holly, as
it is so often symbolic of Christmas time
and the New Year festival.

WINTER HOLLY
STRANDED COTTONS

COLOUR	DMC	ANCHOR	MADEIRA	SKEINS
Coral	351	10	0214	3
Red	666	9046	0210	1
Green	988	257	1402	1
Dark green	986	246	1313	1

COATS OPHIR GOLD THREAD		REELS
Gold	300	1

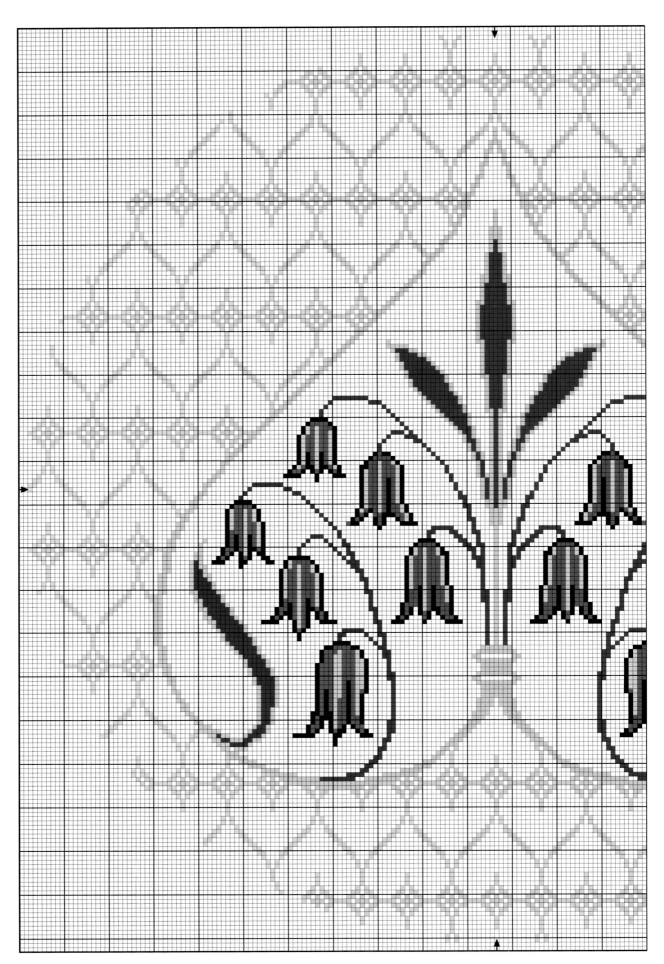

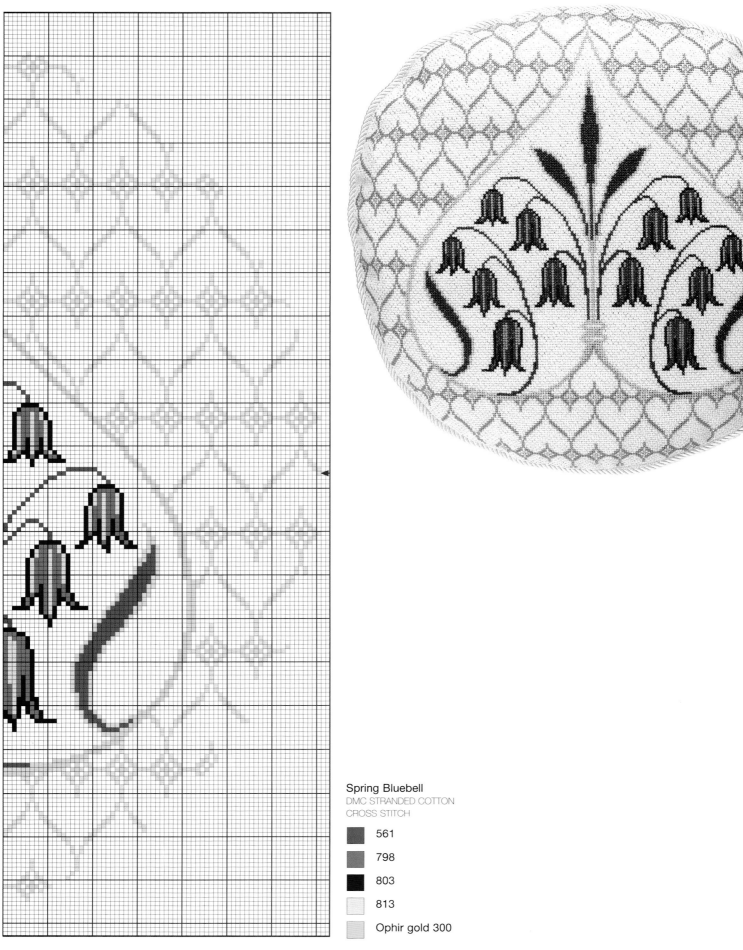

Spring Bluebell

DMC STRANDED COTTON
CROSS STITCH

561

798

803

813

Ophir gold 300

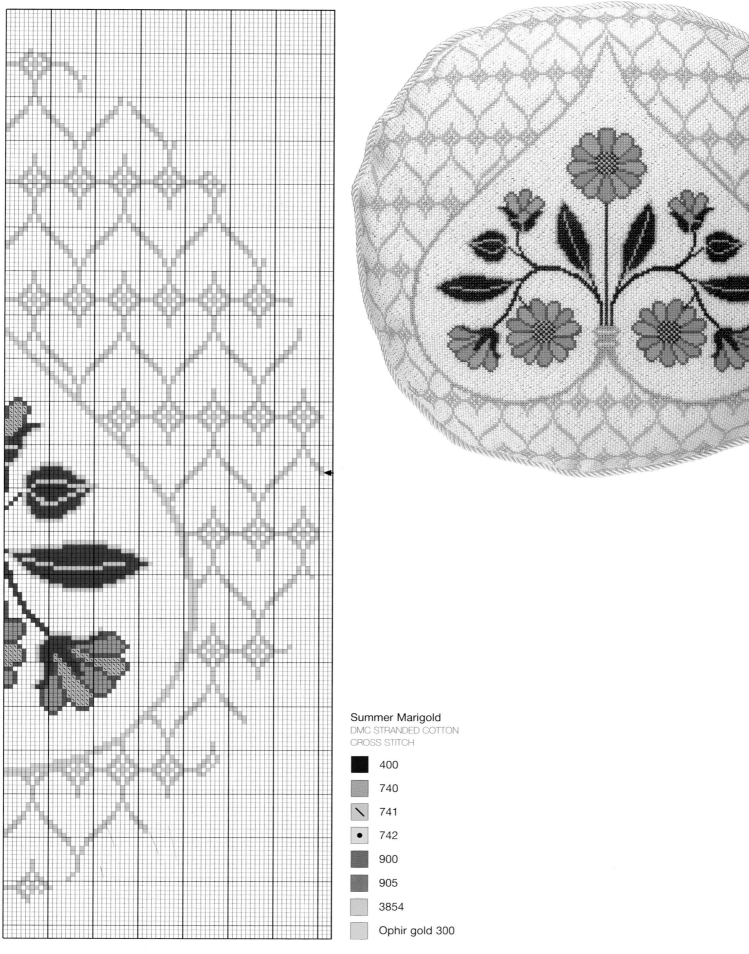

Summer Marigold
DMC STRANDED COTTON
CROSS STITCH

■	400
▨	740
◣	741
•	742
▨	900
▨	905
▨	3854
▨	Ophir gold 300

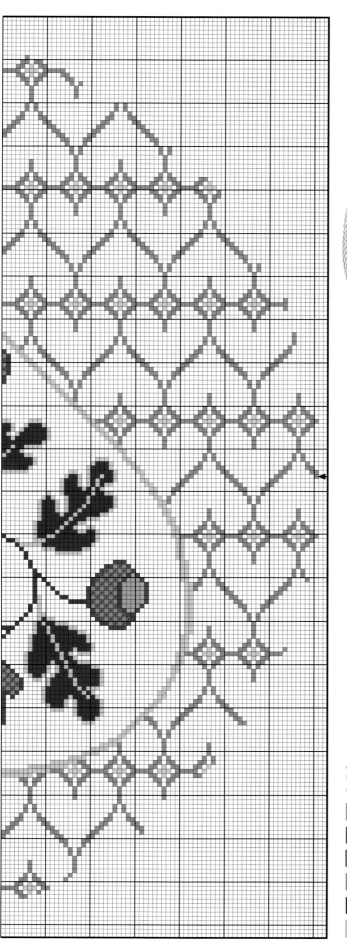

Autumn Acorn
DMC STRANDED COTTON
CROSS STITCH

 436

780

/ 831

832

904

Ophir gold 300

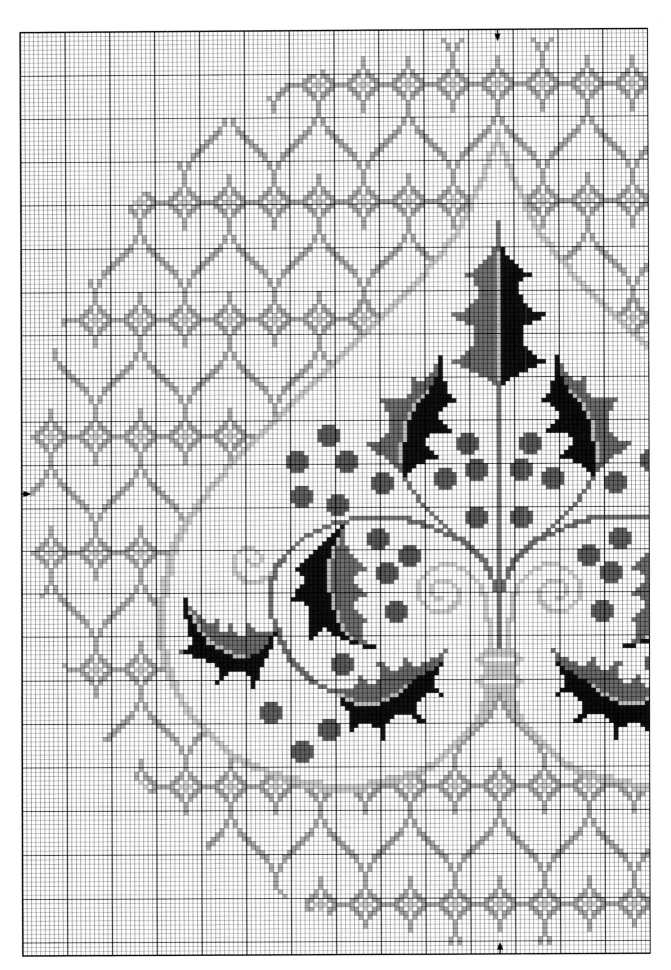

Winter Holly
DMC STRANDED COTTON
CROSS STITCH

	351
	666
	986
	988
	Ophir gold 300

KNOT GARDEN COLLECTION

Knot gardens originated in the Tudor period, influenced by examples from the great houses of France and Italy. These gardens exploited nature, disciplined, trained and clipped it to create clever patterns or mazes on the ground which could be admired from house windows.

Late in the 16th century printed garden manuals began to appear, beginning with Thomas Hill's *A Most Briefe and Plesaunte*  *Treatyse, Teachynge How to Dresse, Sowe, and Set a Garden.* My Tudor garden design (overleaf) is taken from its title page. The blackwork version on page 49 shares the same layout. The knots in instruction books were also recommended to embroiderers, metalworkers and woodworkers.

Planting at this time tended to be simple: a continuous hedge of evergreen material was essential as flowering plants were limited, with short flowering seasons. Plants recommended for hedges included lavender, hyssop, thyme, germander, rue, rosemary, sage and, later, box. A description of  Henry VIII's garden at Hampton Court Palace includes knots, topiary and emblematic shapes made by filling recesses in the ground with coloured materials such as brick dust or chalk.

Heart shapes were extremely popular in Elizabethan times. My heart knot design on page 54 came from *A Short Instruction Verie Profitable and Necessarie for all those that Delight in Gardening*, first published in London in 1591. The circular knot design on page 53 derives from an Elizabethan embroidery and is also composed of a single continuous line.

Three different treatments of the knot garden are illustrated here – the possible colour combinations are endless.

Tudor Garden Box

STITCH COUNT
114 x 114
DESIGN SIZE
20.5 x 20.5cm (8⅛ x 8⅛in) approx

MATERIALS
32 x 32cm (12½ x 12½in)
14-count black Aida
•
Tapestry needle size 26
and a beading needle
•
Stranded cotton (floss) as listed
•
Mill Hill seed beads as listed
•
Oak box with 20cm (8in) square pad
(from Riverbank Woodcrafts,
see Suppliers)

1 Prepare the fabric and mark the centre lines with tacking (basting) (see page 97).

2 Work outwards from the centre of the fabric and the centre of the chart on page 50/51 over one block of Aida, using two strands of stranded cotton (floss) for the cross stitch.

3 Stitch on the beads using one strand of matching thread and a half cross stitch. The frosted white beads represent splashes of water.

4 Remove guidelines and press using a thick towelling layer (see page 97). Mount in the box by removing the pad and stretching the embroidery over it (see page 101).

STRANDED COTTONS

COLOUR	DMC	ANCHOR	MADEIRA	SKEINS
Christmas green	700	229	1304	2
Misty green	3817	875	1209	1
Dark green	905	257	1412	1
Pearl grey	762	234	1804	1
Bright green	703	238	1307	1
Plum pink	3688	1016	0605	1
Steel grey	318	399	1802	1
Yellow green	3819	279	1414	1
Dark blue green	3808	170	1108	1

MILL HILL SEED BEADS

COLOUR	DMC	PACKS
Pink	02005	1
Frosted green	00167	1
Frosted lavender	62047	1
Lavender pink	02082	1
Frosted white	62010	1

Tudor gardens often had Cyprus trees in urns at the centre, but in this design there is a fountain. Circling this are tulip-shaped beds filled with flowering plants, with evergreen beds in between. Around these are grey beds of cotton lavender followed by lavender and outer borders of evergreens. Circular flower beds decorate the corners.

Blackwork Box

STITCH COUNT
112 x 112
DESIGN SIZE
20.5 x 20.5cm (8 x 8in) approx

MATERIALS
63 x 32cm (25 x 12½in)
28-count antique white Quaker cloth
(Zweigart code 101)
•
Stranded cotton (floss) *or* black silk
as listed (from Leon Conrad,
see Suppliers)
•
Mill Hill seed beads as listed
•
Tapestry needle size 26
and a beading needle
•
Gold thread to sew on beads
•
Oak box with 20cm (8in) square pad
(from Riverbank Woodcrafts,
see Suppliers)

1 Prepare the fabric and mark the centre lines with tacking (basting) (see page 97). Work from the chart on page 52 over two fabric threads. Begin stitching the outlines with the thicker silk (or two strands of stranded cotton), outlining the beds using backstitch or double running stitch (see page 98). Check the number of stitches carefully to avoid unpicking.

2 Work the patterns – most are stitched with thin black silk or one strand of cotton (floss) but check line thicknesses carefully. Fasten thread off when moving from one bed to another to avoid it showing on the front.

3 When all blackwork is complete, add the gold seed beads using one strand of gold thread and a half cross stitch.

4 Remove guidelines and press using a thick towelling layer (see page 97). Mount in the box by removing the pad and stretching the embroidery over it (see page 101).

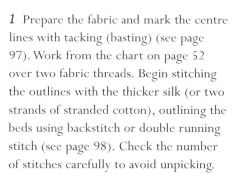

STRANDED COTTONS

COLOUR	DMC	ANCHOR	MADEIRA	SKEINS
Black	310	403	black	3

OR

SILKS EBONY COLLECTION

COLOUR		REELS
Mystery	#540	2
Soft Granite	#270	3

MILL SEED BEADS

COLOUR		PACKS
Gold	02011	1

This variation of the Tudor garden box features different blackwork patterns. Blackwork was a technique that flowered in the Tudor years. It was used to decorate linens and costumes and many Tudor portraits show marvellous examples of whole sleeves in blackwork. Traditionally, it was worked in silks on linen, so for an authentic appearance, use black silks. Original blackwork often included gold or silver threads or spangles made from silver gilt. I have used gold beads.

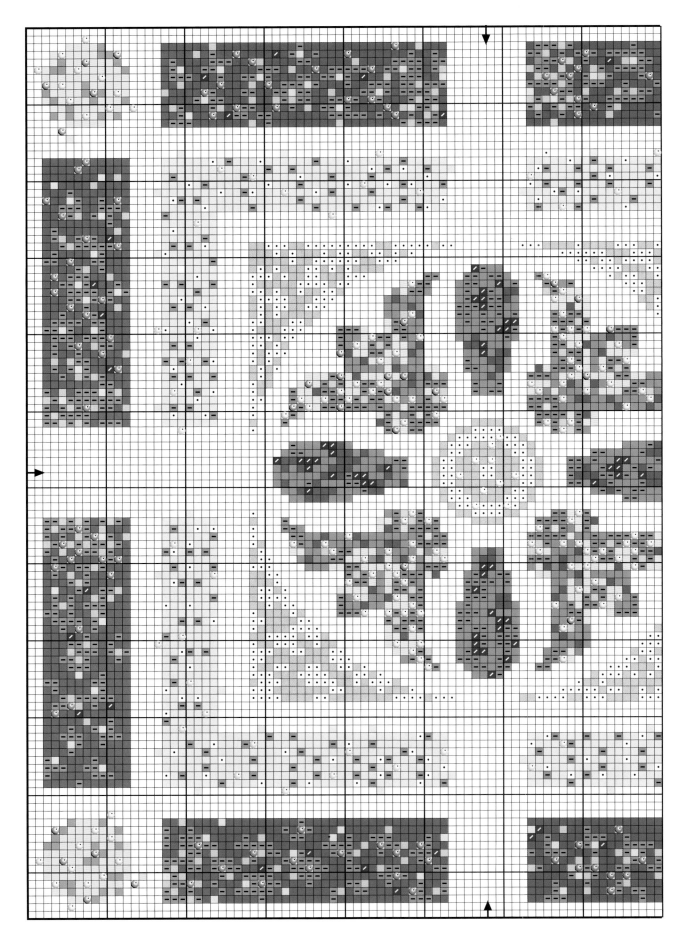

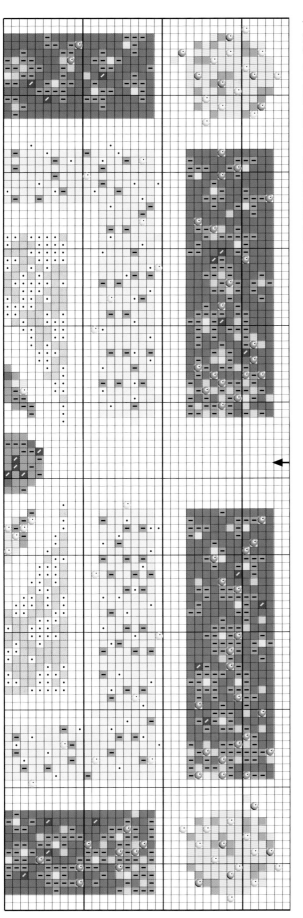

Tudor Garden Box
DMC STRANDED COTTON
CROSS STITCH

	318
	700
	703
•	762
—	905
	3688
/	3808
	3817
	3819

MILL HILL SEED BEADS

- 00167 frosted green
- 02005 pink
- 02082 lavender pink
- 62010 frosted white
- 62047 frosted lavender

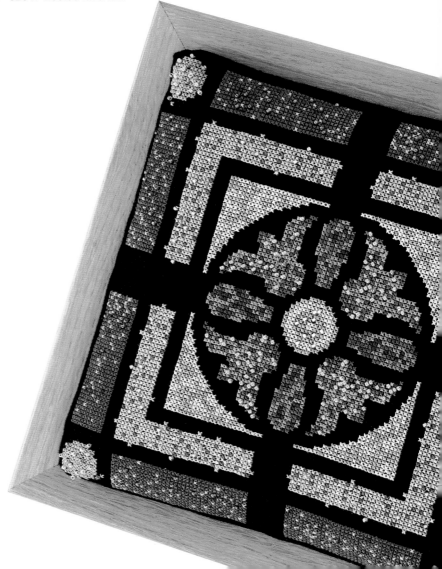

Blackwork Box
BACKSTITCH (OR DOUBLE RUNNING STITCH)

— Mystery 540 silk (or 2 strands black stranded cotton)
— Soft Granite 270 silk (or 1 strand black stranded cotton)

MILL HILL SEED BEADS

⊙ 02011 gold

Circular Knot Box

STITCH COUNT
69 x 69
DESIGN SIZE
11 x 11cm (4½ x 4½in) approx

MATERIALS
23 x 23cm (9 x 9in)
32-count white Belfast linen or
16-count white Aida

•

Tapestry needle size 26

•

Stranded cotton (floss) as listed

•

Circular linen-covered box with
13cm (5in) diameter pad (from
Viking Loom, see Suppliers)

1 Prepare the fabric and mark the centre lines with tacking (basting) (see page 97).

2 Work from the centre of the fabric and the centre of the chart over two threads of linen or over one block of Aida. Use two strands of stranded cotton (floss) for cross stitch and one strand for backstitch.

3 Once all stitching is complete remove any guidelines and press (see page 97). Mount in the box lid by removing the pad and stretching the embroidery over it (see page 101).

STRANDED COTTONS

COLOUR	DMC	ANCHOR	MADEIRA	SKEINS
Light blue	3811	928	1104	1
Mid blue	597	168	1110	1
Dark blue	3808	928	1108	1

Circular Knot Box
DMC STRANDED COTTON
CROSS STITCH

▨	597
■	3808
▢	3811

BACKSTITCH
— 3808

Heart Knot Box

1 Prepare the fabric and mark the centre lines with tacking (basting) (see page 97).

2 Work from the centre of the fabric and the centre of the chart, right, over one block of Aida, using two strands of stranded cotton (floss) for the cross stitch. Take care to keep the stitch direction consistent if you turn the design round as you stitch it.

3 Once all stitching is complete remove any guidelines and press (see page 97). Mount in the box lid by removing the pad and stretching the embroidery over it (see page 101).

I chose this design, with its combination of circle, star, diamond and square, because I like the heart corners. They make a decorative feature that could be used anywhere.

STRANDED COTTONS

COLOUR	DMC	ANCHOR	MADEIRA	SKEINS
Sand	677	886	2207	1
Turquoise	958	187	1114	1
Dark grape	154	970	2604	1
Grape	3835	98	0809	1
Green	3816	876	1207	1
Misty green	3817	875	1209	1
Antique mauve	316	1017	0809	1
Pale mauve	778	1016	0808	1

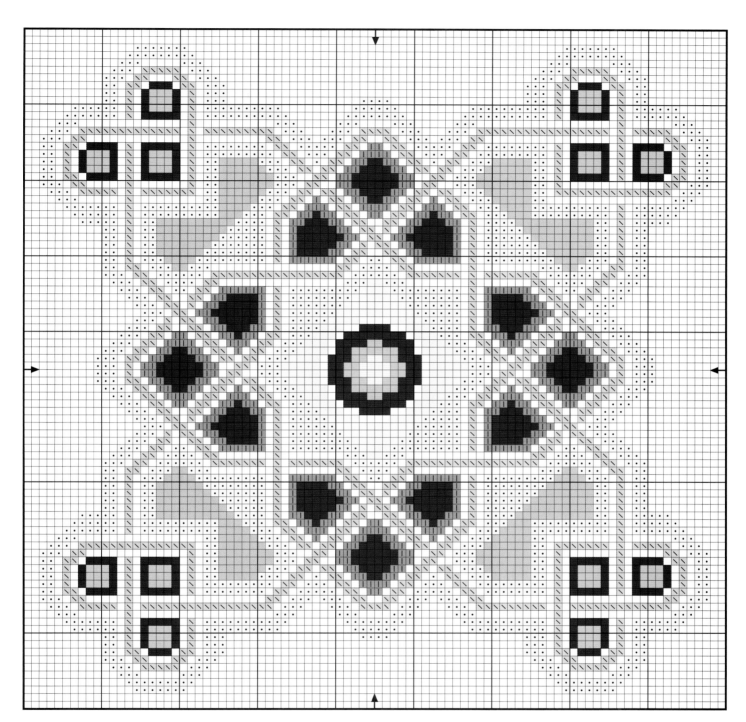

Heart Knot Box
DMC STRANDED COTTON
CROSS STITCH

■	154	╲	958
▨	316	▨	3816
•	677	☐	3817
☐	778	▮	3835

COILING STEM PICTURES

Sleep thou, and I will wind thee in my arms. . .
. . . So doth the woodbine the sweet honeysuckle
Gently entwist;

(From William Shakespeare's *A Midsummer-Night's Dream*, Act IV, Scene i)

These pictures are based on coiling stem patterns with which Tudor and Stuart women decorated their jackets, coifs (head coverings) and cushions, rejoicing in the bright colours of flowers that bloomed for such brief periods but which could be captured in embroidery to cheer house interiors. Adding gold and silver-gilt threads and gold spangles to their work ensured that they caught the light from candles or the big, new Tudor windows.

The coiling patterns were immensely popular and were stitched in blackwork embroidery as well as coloured silks. Blackwork often decorated the caps men wore indoors. Portraits show ladies with whole sleeves embroidered in a similar way. The patterns covered a surface with an evenly spaced series of coils, each containing a flower and perhaps an insect or two. The gleaming gold stems link one coil to another, organized so that the coils form a regular series of rows and columns. The whole surface is covered with a multitude of feasts for the eye as it moves from flower to flower, diverted for a moment by a caterpillar or greedy bird.

The three pictures have captured typical arrangements. The originals, worked in a variety of embroidery stitches, are much smaller than these fragments but I think the cross-stitch versions capture the mood.

The Bird and Borage design (top) features two favourite flowers of embroiderers – the borage and the carnation or gilliflower. We might find the small borage flower

insignificant compared with flowers today (I've shown it bigger than life-size) but at the time its jewel-like shape and medicinal qualities were admired. John Gerard, the medieval herbalist, said the flowers 'exilerate and make the mind glad'. Carnations were a recent import from Europe, much bigger and brighter than the pinks the medieval gardeners had known.

The Peascod and Honeysuckle picture (centre) also shows the new with the old. Honeysuckle, often called woodbine, is an old plant that provided shade and perfume on arbours. Peas were a recent introduction and very fashionable – they crop up frequently in embroidery of this period, often with the peapod worked in detached buttonhole stitch and curled back to reveal the jewelled peas within. They featured in literature as well, Shakespeare calling one of the fairies Peascod in *A Midsummer-Night's Dream*.

The Rose and Thistle picture (below) shows emblematic flowers, the rose signifying England, the thistle Scotland. The two images appear together frequently in early 17th-century embroideries.

It is little wonder that lively and colourful designs such as these were popular during Tudor and Stuart times.
The coils create movement in each picture, enhanced by the use of gleaming metallic gold threads and spangles.

Thistle and Rose

STITCH COUNT
84 x 138
DESIGN SIZE
15.25 x 25cm (6 x 9¾in) approx

MATERIALS
25 x 36cm (10 x 14in)
28-count antique white evenweave
Quaker cloth (Zweigart code 101)
•

Tapestry needle size 26
and a beading needle
•

Stranded cotton (floss) as listed
•

Kreinik Fine (#8) Braid as listed
•

Gold sequins 3mm or 4mm
(see Suppliers)
•

15 x 25cm (6 x 10in)
fusible interfacing

STRANDED COTTONS

COLOUR	DMC	ANCHOR	MADEIRA	SKEINS
Dark green	905	257	1412	1
Green	906	256	1411	1
Pink	3326	36	0606	1
Darker pink	335	38	0610	1
Pale thistle mauve	3836	66	0813	1
Darker thistle mauve	3835	98	0712	1
Terracotta	356	1013	0402	1
Dark terracotta	355	1014	0401	1
Ecru	ecru	926	ecru	1
Yellow	725	305	0106	1
Orange	740	316	0202	1
Black	310	403	black	1
Blue grey	926	850	1707	1

KREINIK FINE (#8) BRAID

COLOUR		REELS
Gold	002HL	2

1 Prepare the fabric and mark the centre lines using tacking (basting) (see page 97). Mount the fabric on an embroidery frame because it may distort, especially when using gold thread.

2 Follow the chart, working over two fabric threads and using two strands of stranded cotton (floss) for the cross stitch and single lengths of the fine braid. Work the gold stem first using the fine braid. Embroider the cross stitch before adding the backstitch details. Use only a single strand for the antennae of the insects. Some of the backstitches charted over several squares at an angle are best worked as long straight stitches.

3 Using a single strand of yellow, stitch on the sequins using a half cross stitch in the direction of your top part of a cross stitch. Take the thread through the sequin as you complete the stitch.

4 When the embroidery is complete remove the guidelines. Remove from the frame and press the work over a layer of towels using a very moderate heat and a pressing cloth – the sequins will distort if heated too much. The historic examples used silver-gilt metal for their 'spangles' but our plastic ones keep their shine because they do not tarnish. Frame as a picture (see page 99 for advice).

Thistle and Rose
DMC STRANDED COTTON
CROSS STITCH

310	356	905
335	725	906
355	740	926

3326	3835
3836	

● ecru
✕ Kreinik 002HL

◎ Gold sequins

BACKSTITCH
— 310 (1 strand)
▬ 310 (2 strands)
▮ 355 (2 strands)
▬ Kreinik 002HL

Bird and Borage

STITCH COUNT
83 x 138

DESIGN SIZE
15.25 x 25cm (6 x 9¾in) approx

MATERIALS
25 x 36cm (10 x 14in) 28-count
antique white evenweave
Quaker cloth (Zweigart code 101)

•

Tapestry needle size 26
and a beading needle

•

Stranded cotton (floss) as listed

•

Kreinik Fine (#8) Braid as listed

•

Gold sequins 3mm or 4mm
(see Suppliers)

•

15 x 25cm (6 x 10in)
fusible interfacing

STRANDED COTTONS

COLOUR	DMC	ANCHOR	MADEIRA	SKEINS
Green	906	256	1411	1
Jade green	992	186	1202	1
Blue	799	145	0910	1
Dark blue	798	137	0911	1
Pale pink	3326	36	0606	1
Pink	335	38	0610	1
Dark rose pink	3350	69	0603	1
Yellow	725	305	0106	1
Dark yellow	972	298	0107	1
Dark gold	782	901	2212	1
Antique violet	3042	870	0807	1
Off white	746	386	0101	1
Black	310	403	black	1

KREINIK FINE (#8) BRAID

COLOUR		REELS
Gold	002HL	2

1 Stitch the bird and borage picture by referring to the instructions on page 58, steps 1–3.

2 When the embroidery is complete remove the guidelines and press carefully, then frame as a picture (see page 99 for advice).

Any of the three coiling stem designs could be made into a central panel for a sumptuous cushion edged with tasselled braid.

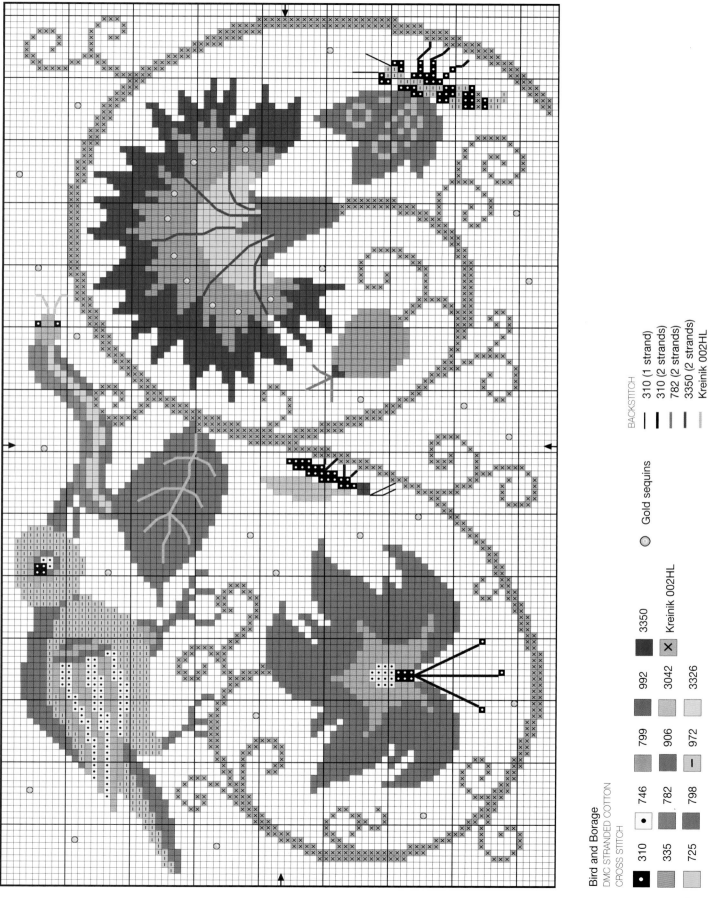

Bird and Borage

DMC STRANDED COTTON

CROSS STITCH

310	746	799	992	3350
335	782	906	3042	Kreinik 002HL
725	798	972	3326	

⦿ Gold sequins

BACKSTITCH

	310 (1 strand)
	310 (2 strands)
	782 (2 strands)
	3350 (2 strands)
	Kreinik 002HL

Peascod and Honeysuckle

STITCH COUNT
84 x 138
DESIGN SIZE
15.25 x 25cm (6 x 9¾in) approx

MATERIALS
25 x 36cm (10 x 14in)
28-count antique white evenweave
Quaker cloth (Zweigart code 101)
•
Tapestry needle size 26
and a beading needle
•
Stranded cotton (floss) as listed
•
Kreinik Fine (#8) Braid as listed
•
Gold sequins 3mm or 4mm
(see Suppliers)
•
15 x 25cm (6 x 10in)
fusible interfacing

STRANDED COTTONS

COLOUR	DMC	ANCHOR	MADEIRA	SKEINS
Green	906	256	1411	1
Dark green	905	257	1412	1
Dark blue	798	137	0911	1
Pink	352	9	0303	1
Dark coral	349	13	0212	1
Dark terracotta	355	1014	0401	1
Off white	746	386	0101	1
Beige	738	942	2013	1
Pale yellow	727	293	0110	1
Yellow	725	305	0106	1
Dark gold	782	901	2212	1
Light grey green	927	849	2013	1
Grey green	3768	851	1706	1
Black	310	403	black	1

KREINIK FINE (#8) BRAID

COLOUR		REELS
Gold	002HL	2

1 Stitch the peacod and honeysuckle picture by referring to the instructions on page 58, steps 1–3.

2 When the embroidery is complete remove the guidelines and press carefully, then frame as a picture (see page 99 for advice).

This design, or either of the other two coiling stems designs, could be made up into an attractive book cover, especially as a gift for a gardening friend.

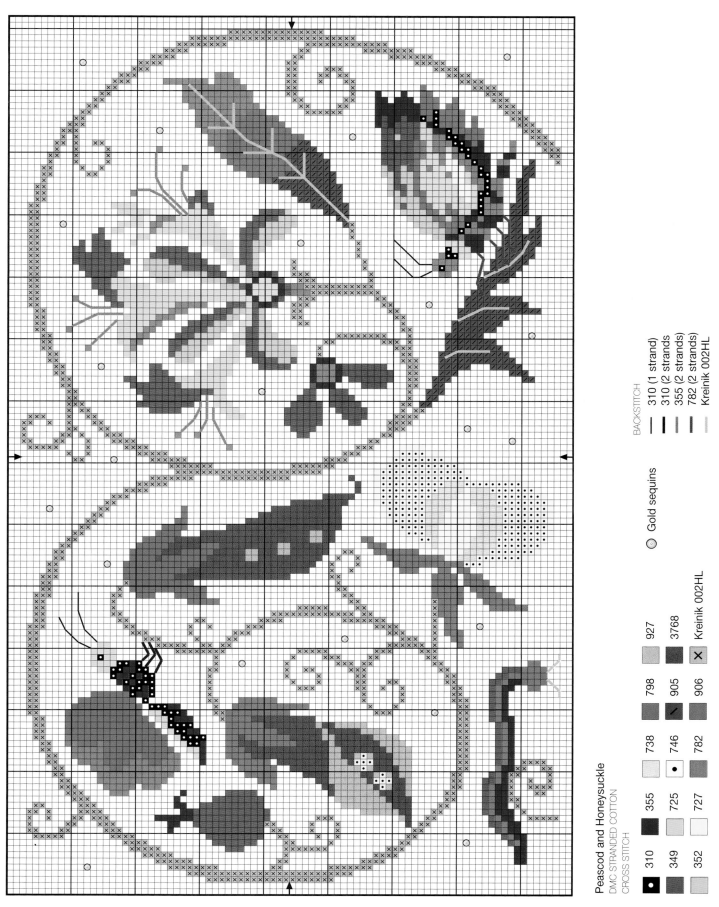

Peascod and Honeysuckle
DMC STRANDED COTTON
CROSS STITCH

310		355		738		927
349		725		798		3768
352		727		746		Kreinik 002HL
				905		
				782		
				906		

◎ Gold sequins

BACKSTITCH

—— 310 (1 strand)
—— 310 (2 strands)
—— 355 (2 strands)
—— 782 (2 strands)
—— Kreinik 002HL

BOUNTIFUL TREE
FIRESCREEN

This astonishing tree, bearing all sorts of fruits and nuts, is based on one embroidered in silks during the early 17th century (now in the Metropolitan Museum of Art, New York). Embroidered pictures became popular around this time, many of them showing biblical stories, though the figures were set in English countryside and dressed in contemporary costume. Whatever the subject matter, the background was used as an opportunity to include all sorts of flora and fauna, ranging from elephants, lions, leopards, camels, stags, unicorns and dogs to mermaids, kingfishers, fish, owls, squirrels, rabbits, snails, caterpillars, moths, grasshoppers, parrots and many other birds.

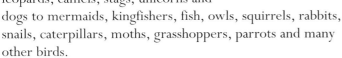

One of the favourite subjects was the Garden of Eden, a paradise garden in a state of perfection. It often included Adam and Eve and the Serpent and, of course, a fruiting tree bearing the fruit of the knowledge of good and evil. At the time there was great enthusiasm for gardening. Books of advice were being printed which included explanation, with diagrams, of how to graft desirable fruits on to commonplace trees. With a little imagination, the tree in the embroidery can be seen as a common crab apple with apples, pears, figs, pomegranates, plums, oranges and

lemons grafted on to it. It is more difficult to imagine the strawberries growing in the same way, but the embroiderer clearly wanted to include everything that was delicious. The difference in the leaves (notice the recognisable fig leaves and oak leaves) supports the idea of grafting.

All around the tree in the original embroidery were different plants, birds, animals and insects – domestic, foreign and mythical. In front of the tree flows a river with different varieties of fish. The flowers that are spotted around the tree would have been 'slips' in the original embroidery. That was the name for small pieces of embroidery, often copied from Herbals, which were stitched on fine canvas and then cut out and applied to another piece by stitching round the edges. More examples can be seen in the Motif Library beginning on page 85.

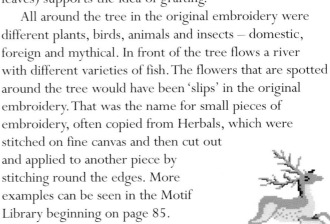

The tree in my firescreen is a somewhat simplified version of the inspirational original – I simply could not find room for the goat, unicorn and pheasant! I have, however, included a great range of fruit, berries and nuts, and a grape vine twisting round the tree trunk. To show such a diversity of objects using whole cross stitches and a manageable number of colours was a real challenge.

This magnificent tree makes an impressive firescreen or picture. If you do not want to stitch the whole scene you will find it a treasury of details for small projects or cards.

Bountiful Tree Firescreen

1 Prepare the fabric and mark the centre lines with tacking (basting) (see page 97). This is quite a large design so I suggest adding extra guidelines every 20 squares, working outwards from the centre lines.

2 Work from the centre of the fabric and the centre of the chart on pages 68–73 over one block of Aida using two strands of stranded cotton (floss) for the cross stitch. Refer to the chart for the backstitch colours and number of strands to use.

3 Begin cross stitching the tree trunk: as you embroider the branches, the skeleton of the design will become clear. Work the remaining motifs from the centre out, checking their positions carefully.

4 When the embroidery is complete, remove guidelines and press (see page 97). Refer to page 99 for stretching work over mount board and then mount in the firescreen according to the manufacturer's instructions.

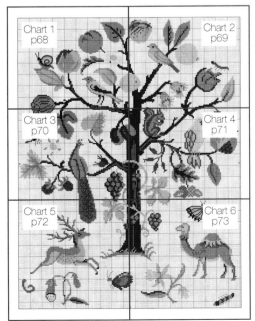

The firescreen chart is split over six pages (pages 68–73), with the whole design shown here. For your own use you could colour photocopy the chart parts, enlarging them if you wish, and tape them all together.

STRANDED COTTONS

COLOUR	DMC	ANCHOR	MADEIRA	SKEINS
Lightest green	3348	254	1409	1
Light green	704	256	1308	2
Green	905	257	1412	2
Dark green	3345	263	1405	1
Very light emerald	955	206	1210	1
Light emerald	913	204	1212	1
Emerald green	911	230	0301	1
Dark emerald	3818	923	1303	1
Lemon	444	297	0105	1
Yellow	743	305	0113	1
Primrose	727	293	0110	1
Orange	721	324	0308	1
Copper	920	1004	0312	1
Golden brown	977	1002	2307	1
Light brown	435	1046	2010	1
Brown	433	371	2008	2
Dark brown	938	380	2005	1
Cream	712	926	2101	1
Beige	842	388	1910	1
Grey	452	232	1807	1
Light tan	738	942	2013	1
Tan	436	1045	2011	1
Mauve	316	1017	0809	1
Dark grape	3834	970	2614	1
Dark coral	817	46	0211	1
Garnet	902	897	0601	1

Chart 1

Bountiful Tree Firescreen
DMC STRANDED COTTON
CROSS STITCH

▨ 316	╱ 712	▬ 902	• 977	
■ 433	T 721	▨ 905	╱ 3345	
L 435	Z 727	V 911	╲ 3348	
▨ 436	738	O 913	▨ 3818	
444	I 743	X 920	▨ 3824	
N 452	817	• 938		
704	▬ 842	955		

BACKSTITCH (STRANDS)

▬	433	(1)
▬	433	(2)
▬	435	(1)
▬	435	(2)
▬	436	(1)
▬	911	(1)
▬	938	(2)
▬	3345	(1)
▬	3818	(1)
▬	3834	(1)

Chart 2

435 (1)

435 (1)

Chart 3

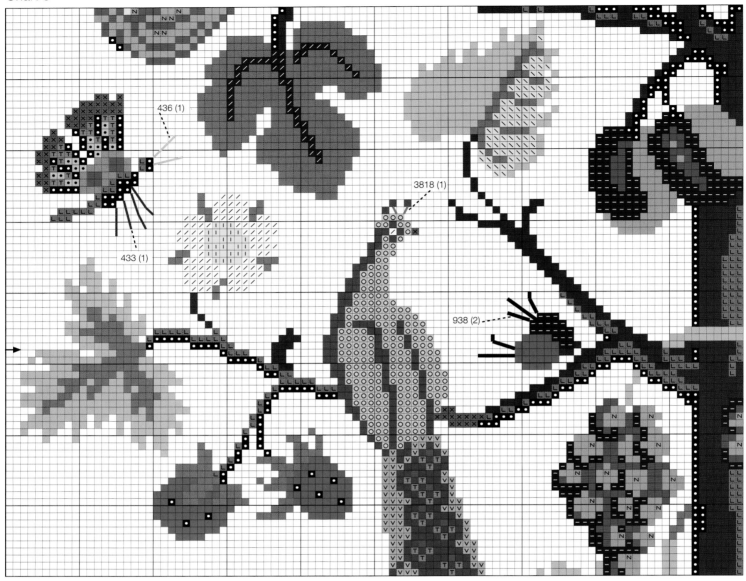

Bountiful Tree Firescreen

DMC STRANDED COTTON
CROSS STITCH

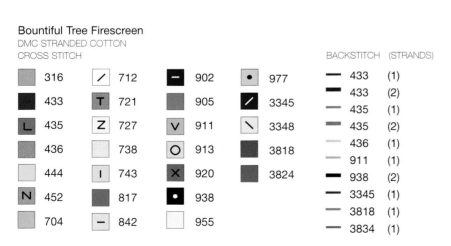

	316	/	712	–	902	•	977	
	433	T	721		905	/	3345	
L	435	Z	727	V	911	\	3348	
	436		738	O	913		3818	
	444	I	743	X	920		3824	
N	452		817	•	938			
	704	–	842		955			

BACKSTITCH (STRANDS)

—	433	(1)
—	433	(2)
—	435	(1)
—	435	(2)
—	436	(1)
—	911	(1)
—	938	(2)
—	3345	(1)
—	3818	(1)
—	3834	(1)

Chart 4

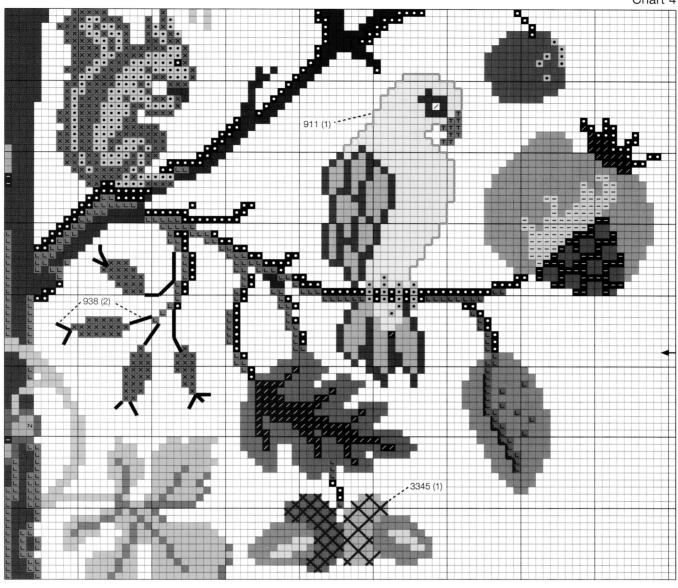

911 (1)

938 (2)

3345 (1)

Chart 5

3834 (1)

433 (2)

911 (1)

3834 (1)

Bountiful Tree Firescreen
DMC STRANDED COTTON
CROSS STITCH

	316	/	712	−	902	•	977	
	433	T	721		905	/	3345	
L	435	Z	727	V	911	\	3348	
	436		738	O	913		3818	
	444	I	743	X	920		3824	
N	452		817	•	938			
	704	−	842		955			

BACKSTITCH (STRANDS)

—	433	(1)
—	433	(2)
—	435	(1)
—	435	(2)
—	436	(1)
—	911	(1)
—	938	(2)
—	3345	(1)
—	3818	(1)
—	3834	(1)

Chart 6

435 (2)

938 (2)

3834 (1)

SWETE BAGGES

She prizes not such trifles as these are:
The gifts she looks from me are pack'd and lock'd
Up in my heart, which I have given already,
But not deliver'd.

(From William Shakespeare's *The Winter's Tale*, Act IV, Scene iv)

*I*n the Tudor period little drawstring bags were made to contain gifts – perfume, money or marzipan confectionery. The bags were lavishly embroidered, often with gold and silver thread and embellished with seed pearls, and many had matching pincushions – pins being very necessary for securing costumes at that time. At the court of Queen Elizabeth, courtiers presented gifts to the Queen at New Year, a custom continued by the Stuart monarchs.

The bags in this section were inspired by the Tudor examples. You could use them to hold precious possessions or, as the originals may have been, to protect treasured books. The green bag with its stag, carnation, roses, acorns and mistletoe is a cross-stitch version of a lavish Tudor original. 'Pearl' beads are used in imitation of the original. Its accompanying pincushion features a rose.

The black bag has flowers, pomegranates and acorns within a silver interlocked framework. One flower has been selected for the pincushion but any could be used.

The technique used on the blue bag was prompted by the love of bead embroidery during the period. The design of two birds on a fountain is from a 'lacis' hanging, made from lots of squares joined together. Lacis is a whitework technique where net is darned to  create solid areas. It was one of the embroidery techniques that Mary Queen of Scots practised to while away her imprisonment. This design and its pincushion could either be cross stitched or embroidered with beads.

These beautiful bags have been trimmed with beads and tassels, as the originals would have been. The pincushion designs could be used for little purses, coasters, cards or scented sachets.

Rose Bag

STITCH COUNT
115 x 110

DESIGN SIZE
21 x 19.5cm (8¼ x 7¾in) approx

MATERIALS

38 x 28cm (15 x 11in) 14-count green Aida (Fabric Flair N14.626)

•

Tapestry needle size 26 and a beading needle

•

Stranded cotton (floss) as listed

•

Mill Hill seed beads as listed

•

28 x 38cm (11 x 15in) fabric for the back

•

Two pieces 25 x 36cm (10 x 14in) lining fabric

•

Two pieces 25 x 36cm (10 x 14in) fusible interfacing

•

Eyelets and eyelet tool (optional)

•

Cord for drawstrings and handle 1.5m (1½yd) approx

The bag design would make an attractive picture: the red bordering lines could be stitched all round the design or omitted altogether.

1 Prepare the fabric by folding back 5cm (2in) at the top. On the lower part find the centre horizontal and vertical lines and mark with tacking (basting).

2 Follow the chart, beginning near the centre, using two strands of stranded cotton (floss) for cross stitch. Start with the carnation and then embroider the blue stems to help locate all the rest.

3 Sew on the beads using a single strand of matching cotton (floss) and a beading needle with half or full cross stitch. Make sure the beads face the same direction.

4 When the embroidery is complete remove guide lines and press from the back with several layers of towelling underneath. Iron a piece of interfacing on to the back of the embroidery and another onto the fabric for the back of the bag. Place the embroidered fabric and the bag back, right sides together, and

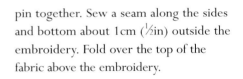

pin together. Sew a seam along the sides and bottom about 1cm (½in) outside the embroidery. Fold over the top of the fabric above the embroidery.

5 Using the lining fabric, make a bag shape that can be hand sewn to the folded area at the top of the bag, 4cm (1½in) from the fold. Position six eyelets at the top of the front, punching them through the double layer. Repeat with the back of the bag. Alternatively, cut holes and neaten them with stitches.

6 Cut the cord into three lengths. Thread one length through the eyelets from the left all the way round and knot the cord at the left side. Repeat with the second length of cord, starting from the right. Add a bead or tassel on the ends if desired.

7 Sew the third length of cord to either side of the bag for a handle. You could use different cord for this if you prefer.

STRANDED COTTONS

COLOUR	DMC	ANCHOR	MADEIRA	SKEINS
Red	3831	42	0507	1
Pink	3733	66	0605	1
Green	3813	875	1702	1
Light blue	598	167	1111	1
Soft white	3865	2	white	1
Brown	437	362	2012	1
Yellow	725	305	0106	1

MILL HILL SEED BEADS

Cream	00123
Pink	02005

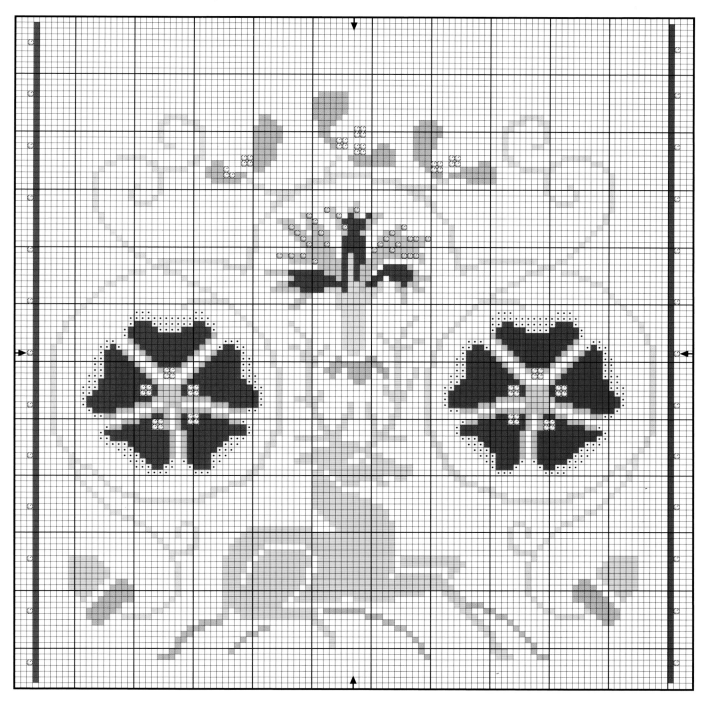

Rose Bag

DMC STRANDED COTTON
CROSS STITCH

MILL HILL SEED BEADS

☐ 437	☐ 3813	◉ 00123 cream
☐ 598	■ 3831	◉ 02005 pink
☐ 725	⦁ 3865	
☐ 3733		

Gilliflower Bag

STITCH COUNT
109 x 103
DESIGN SIZE
10 x 9cm (7¾ x 7¼in) approx

MATERIALS
28 x 38cm (11 x 15in)
14-count black Aida
•
Tapestry needle size 26
•
Stranded cotton (floss) as listed
•
Kreinik Fine (#8) Braid 001HL
•
28 x 38cm (11 x 15in)
fabric for the back
•
Two pieces 25 x 36cm (10 x 14in)
lining fabric
•
Two pieces 25 x 36cm (10 x 14in)
fusible interfacing
•
Eyelets and eyelet tool (optional)
•
Cord for drawstrings and handle
1.5m (1½yd) approx

STRANDED COTTONS

COLOUR	DMC	ANCHOR	MADEIRA	SKEINS
Red	349	13	0212	1
Pink	603	62	0701	1
Pale pink	605	60	0613	1
Acorn brown	782	901	2212	1
Tan	729	890	2012	1
Green	954	203	1211	1
Yellow	726	293	0110	1
Blue	799	145	0910	1
Dark blue	3808	170	1108	1

KREINIK FINE (#8) BRAID

COLOUR		REELS
Silver	001HL	4

1 Prepare the fabric as described on page 76, step 1.

2 Follow the chart, beginning near the centre, using two strands of stranded cotton (floss) and a single strand of fine braid for cross stitches. Embroider the silver network first, and then work the fruit, acorns and flowers in the spaces.

3 To make up the bag, follow steps 4–7 on page 76. If desired, you could add silver beads to the cord and fray the ends into little tassels.

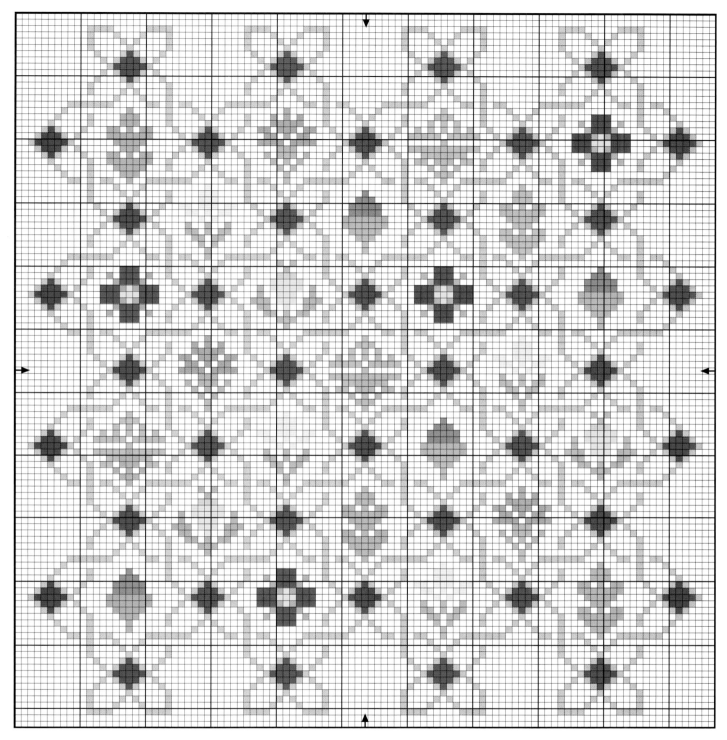

Gilliflower Bag
DMC STRANDED COTTON
CROSS STITCH

▦	349	▦	782
▦	603	▦	799
▦	605	▦	954
▦	726	▦	3808
▦	729	▦	Kreinik Fine Braid (#8) 001HL

Beaded Bag

STITCH COUNT
80 x 80
DESIGN SIZE
14.5 x 14.5cm (5¾ x 5¾in) approx
MATERIALS
28 x 38cm (11 x 15in) 14-count
blue Aida (Zweigart code 594)

•

Size 26 tapestry needle
and a beading needle

•

Mill Hill seed beads: 3 packs cream
00123 and 2 packs grey 00150

•

28 x 38cm (11 x 15in)
fabric for the back

•

Two pieces 25 x 36cm (10 x 14in)
lining fabric

•

Cream and grey sewing thread

•

Two pieces 25 x 36cm (10 x 14in)
fusible interfacing

•

Eyelets and eyelet tool (optional)

•

Cord for drawstrings and handle
1.5m (1½yd) approx

1 Prepare the fabric as step 1, page 76. It may be easier to stitch this design with the help of an embroidery frame.

2 Follow the chart, beginning stitching near the centre using a beading needle and cream sewing thread. Make a knot and then a double stitch to secure. Sew on the cream beads using a half cross stitch through each bead. Every two or three beads take a few stitches on the back of the fabric to keep the tension taut. Take care to keep checking the number of beads and comparing it to the chart. When you have completed the

This delicately coloured bag design would make a lovely scented sachet filled with sweet-smelling pot-pourri.

birds, fountain and flowers, change to grey sewing thread and grey beads and work the border.

3 To make up the bag, follow steps 4–7 on page 76 but use a 3.5cm (1½in) seam. If desired, you could add silver beads to the cord and fray the ends into little tassels.

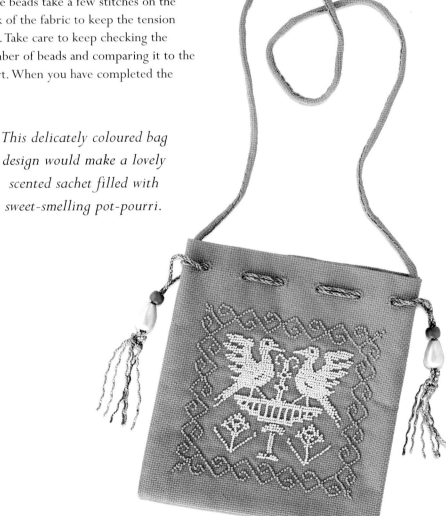

Beaded Bag
MILL HILL SEED BEADS

⊙ 00123 cream

⊙ 00150 grey

Rose Pincushion

STITCH COUNT
48 x 48
DESIGN SIZE
9 x 9cm (3½ x 3½in) approx

MATERIALS
20 x 20cm (8 x 8in) 14-count
green Aida (Fabric Flair N14.626)
•
Tapestry needle size 26
•
Stranded cotton (floss) as listed
•
Scrap of fabric for the back
•
Polyester filling

1 Prepare the fabric and mark the centre lines with tacking (basting).

2 Follow the chart, cross stitching from the centre out, using two strands of stranded cotton (floss) throughout.

3 When the embroidery is complete remove guide lines and press. Make up as a pincushion (see page 101). Add tassels at the corners if required (see page 101).

STRANDED COTTONS

COLOUR	DMC	ANCHOR	MADEIRA	SKEINS
Red	3831	42	0507	1
Pink	3733	66	0605	1
Green	3813	875	1702	1
Light blue	598	167	1111	1
Soft white	3865	2	white	1
Brown	437	362	2012	1
Yellow	725	305	0106	1

If you have already made the rose bag, you may have enough thread left over for this matching pincushion. Soft white replaces the cream beads on the bag.

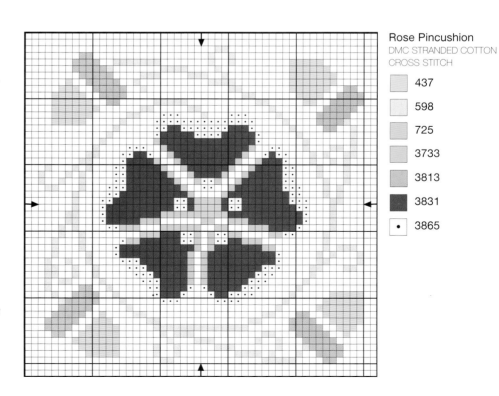

Rose Pincushion
DMC STRANDED COTTON
CROSS STITCH

▨	437
▨	598
▨	725
▨	3733
▨	3813
▨	3831
•	3865

Gillifower Pincushion

STITCH COUNT
31 x 31

DESIGN SIZE
5.5 x 5.5cm (2¼ x 2¼in) approx

MATERIALS

6 x 6in (15 x 15cm)
14-count black Aida

•

Tapestry needle size 26

•

Stranded cotton (floss) as listed

•

Kreinik Fine (#8) Braid 001HL

•

Scrap of fabric for the back

•

Polyester filling

•

Short length of twisted cord or braid
for handle (optional)

1 Follow steps 1–3 on the opposite page
to stitch and make up this pincushion but
follow the chart below.

2 If desired, add a twisted cord or
braid handle.

STRANDED COTTONS

COLOUR	DMC	ANCHOR	MADEIRA	SKEINS
Pink	603	62	0701	1
Green	954	203	1211	1
Dark blue	3808	170	1108	1

KREINIK FINE (#8) BRAID

COLOUR		REELS
Silver	001HL	4

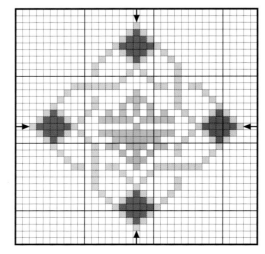

Gilliflower Pincushion
DMC STRANDED COTTON
CROSS STITCH

▨	603
▨	954
▨	3808
▨	Kreinik Fine Braid (#8) 001HL

White Bird Pincushion

1 Follow steps 1–3 on page 82 but use a single strand of ecru perlé cotton throughout or two strands of ecru stranded cotton (floss), following the chart below.

2 If desired, use matching thread to add pearl beads around the edge of the pincushion.

This pincushion design could be worked in beads, as the bag was, and made up as a pretty, matching purse by simply stitching a zip into one side.

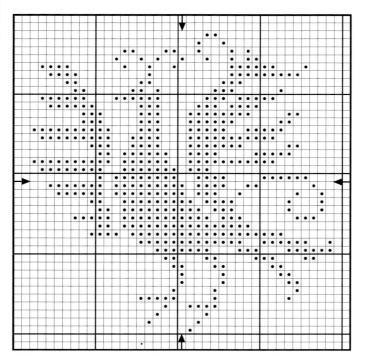

White Bird Pincushion
DMC PERLE COTTON NO.8
CROSS STITCH

• ecru

Motif Library

The following pages show a variety of charted details from Tudor and Stuart needlework which could be used alone on small pieces or be grouped together with your own ideas. Colours are for guidance only.

The lion and the leopard on page 86 have been taken from 'spot' samplers, where a variety of motifs were crowded together. Such a collection was intended to be a reference from which to copy items on to fine linen, cut them out and apply them to larger pieces of work. A dark background was chosen to show up the light colours of hounds and unicorn but is not necessary for the other creatures. Any of these motifs could be used for cards, in the corners of mats or napkins or in larger compositions. The huntsman and his hounds could be rearranged and placed on a hill or by a river. Alternatively, the huntsman and all the hounds could be worked as a long border picture.

The insects on page 89 were originally embroidered on clothes, bed linen, cushions, and samplers. They can be used alone on small items such as fridge magnets or added to almost anything else. The fish could be worked with the mermaid on page 88, as could other flying creatures. The mermaid occurred frequently in decorative work of the early 17th century.

The first design on page 87 was chosen for a bookmark (shown right) and fits on to

This pincushion design (charted on page 94) is from a celebrated late 16th-century sampler. The fruits are enhanced with seed beads.

A unicorn (page 86) tosses its mane and tail, which have been stitched with rayon floss to catch the light in an enchanting way on this card.

standard Aida band, as does the second. The first uses flowers from early samplers, the second is simplified from an Elizabethan border. The pattern on the right comes from a portrait of Sir Philip Sidney of 1577, where it decorated his trunkhose. This could be used as a continuous border for a belt, bag strap or bookmark. The pink and blue design on page 90 could also be used for a bookmark.

The designs on pages 91, 92, 93 and 94 are examples of all-over patterns suitable for cushions, stools, boxes, bags or pincushions. As they are regular repeats you can adapt them to any size. The motifs at the bottom of page 93 show how a detail can be extracted from a bigger picture and used alone.

The strawberries on page 94 would make a lovely cushion: choose the white flower as the centre, surrounded on all sides by the strawberries, or place the strawberries in the centres with flowers in the corners. Try adding beads for the pips.

The elaborate gold border at the top of page 88 could be used at top and (flipped) at bottom, and maybe at the sides of a piece to surround a special treasure or message. The borders on page 95 are all from original samplers and suitable for using separately or for inclusion in your own sampler. The section outlined with a dashed blue line is suitable for substituting for the whitework in the sampler on page 28 and provides a colourful alternative. You can also make your own choice from the borders included on these pages.

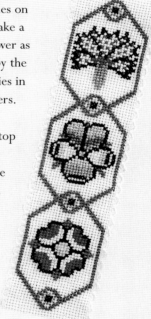

This bookmark (charted on page 87) would make a lovely gift. It shows a carnation, pansy and rose, which featured on early samplers.

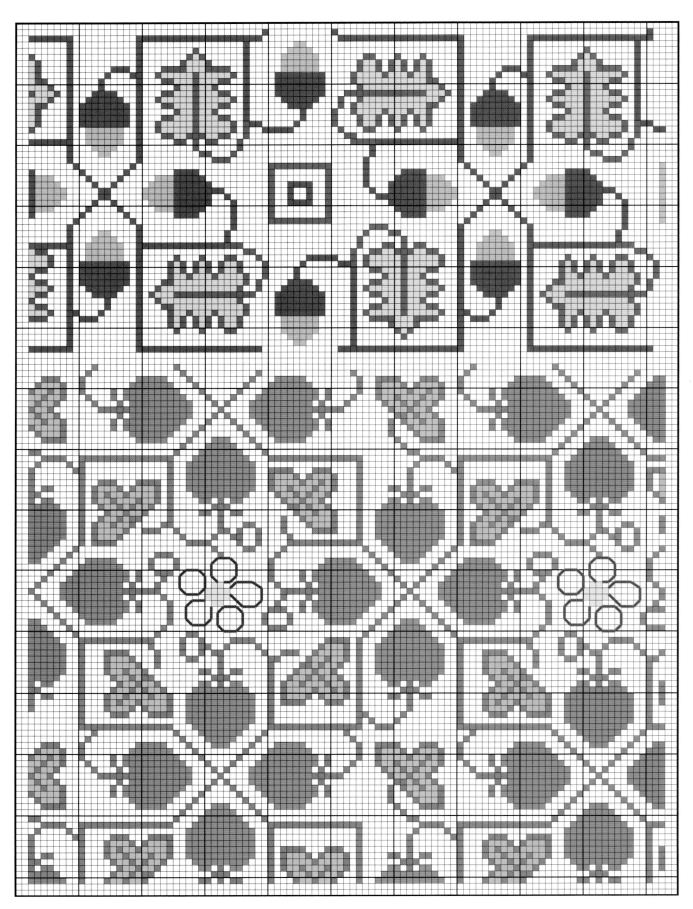

The pattern within the blue dashed lines can be used as an alternative to the whitework section in the band sampler on page 28.

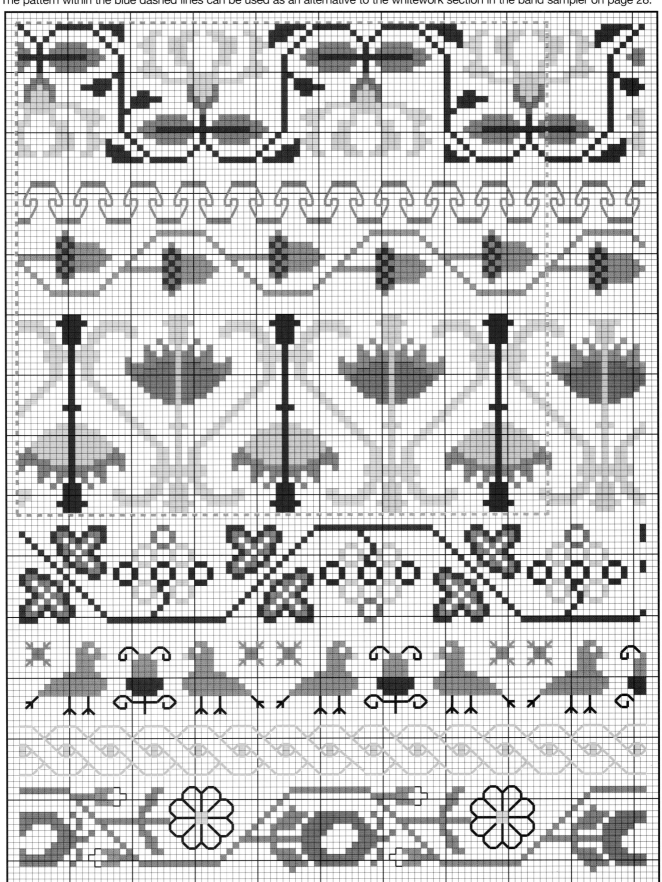

MATERIALS, TECHNIQUES AND STITCHES

This section of the book will be particularly useful to those of you who are new to cross stitch embroidery as it describes the materials and equipment needed, the techniques used and how the stitches are worked.

MATERIALS

Successful cross stitch embroidery requires only basic materials and equipment readily available from good needlecraft shops.

❀ FABRICS ❀

The projects in this book list exactly the fabric required for working the piece as in the photograph but you can, of course, substitute one fabric for another.

Aida is a blockweave fabric which is probably the simplest to work. The weave locks each block of threads in place resulting in a firm, very stable fabric.

Evenweave fabric, such as linen, has the same number of warp and weft threads to 1in or 2.5cm. The gauge is the holes per inch (h.p.i.) or the count. An evenweave is usually embroidered over two threads at a time, an Aida over one block. Thus a 28-count evenweave fabric can be substituted for a 14-count Aida, a 32-count evenweave for a 16-count Aida — and vice versa.

❀ THREADS ❀

STRANDED COTTON (FLOSS) Most of the projects use stranded cottons; I used DMC but if you prefer one of the alternatives given bear in mind that they are not always an exact colour match. The names I have used are for convenience and are not official colour names that manufacturers will recognize. Always order by the number. Divide skeins into lengths of about 50cm (20in) and divide each length into its six strands. Recombine the number needed for cross stitching — usually two.

OPHIR METALLIC THREAD This is made by Coats Crafts and is a three-ply thread twisted together into a single thread. Use as it comes.

EBONY SILK THREADS These are used for the blackwork box on page 49. They are used as single threads and give a sharp, clear line.

METALLIC BRAID Metallic braid is used as it comes from the reel. Work with shorter lengths than usual, about 30cm (12in).

❀ EQUIPMENT ❀

NEEDLES All the embroidery is done with blunt-ended tapestry needles. I have recommended sizes, but you may prefer a size larger or smaller: it is a compromise between having a large enough eye to take the thread and a size of needle that will pass through the fabric holes without too much friction. You will also need a beading needle for sewing on the beads used in some projects.

GENERAL ACCESSORIES Apart from fabric, thread and needles you must have a good pair of embroidery scissors with sharp points, as well as fabric scissors. I think a bright light is essential, preferably with a 'daylight' bulb. When you work on dark fabrics it is really helpful to place a brightly reflective sheet of paper or white pillow slip over your knees to make the holes in the fabric show up much more clearly. You may find that working some of the designs in this book will be much easier with the aid of a magnifier.

FRAMES I recommend using a frame for any evenweave fabric and when working with a mixture of threads as their different characteristics may cause you to pull some threads more firmly than others and thus distort the fabric. For small pieces of embroidery a hoop frame or flexi-hoop will be suitable. Always try to use a frame large enough to take the whole of the design. If this is not possible then only leave the frame on the work whilst you are actually embroidering, and take care when repositioning it not to let the edge coincide with an embroidered area as this could flatten the stitches. Small pieces of Aida are usually firm enough to be worked without a frame. Visit your local needlework shop to see a selection of frames, such as hoops, rectangular 'slate' frames and clip frames.

TECHNIQUES

This section describes the techniques used for stitching the projects in the book,
how to prepare fabric ready for stitching, how to use the charts and how to work the stitches.

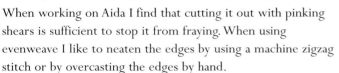

PREPARING THE FABRIC

When working on Aida I find that cutting it out with pinking
shears is sufficient to stop it from fraying. When using
evenweave I like to neaten the edges by using a machine zigzag
stitch or by overcasting the edges by hand.

The centre point on the chart is indicated by the use of
opposing arrows. Find the centre of your fabric by folding it in
half both ways. Mark the centre lines by tacking (basting) with
sewing thread, making sure that the tacked line stays straight
along the grain of the fabric. In some of the larger more
complex designs I have suggested marking extra guidelines –
choose one colour for the centre lines and another for any other
lines. I find a little time spent marking out greatly reduces
counting mistakes.

CALCULATING THE DESIGN SIZE

As you gain confidence you may choose to work on a larger or
smaller grade of fabric. This will of course result in the finished
piece being a different size. To find out how large a piece would
become divide the stitch count given by the number of holes
per 1in (2.5cm) of the fabric (the count). Remember to then
add at least 5cm (2in) extra on all sides to allow for making up
– the fabric amounts listed in the projects allow for this. Where
measurements are given the height is quoted first, followed by
the width.

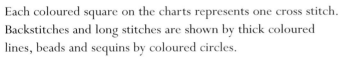

FOLLOWING THE CHARTS

Each coloured square on the charts represents one cross stitch.
Backstitches and long stitches are shown by thick coloured
lines, beads and sequins by coloured circles.

The keys accompanying the charts have the threads used and
their codes, while the thread lists within the projects include
alternatives to DMC stranded cotton (floss) where appropriate.
Where necessary, symbols have been added to aid colour
identification. The charts have slightly more pronounced lines
every ten squares to help with counting.

You can use the charts straight from the book or photocopy
them in colour for your own use. This allows you to enlarge and
tape together sections of the larger charts. If you do this then
you can cross off areas as you work them, which some people
find helpful. It also allows you to draw in the centre lines and
any extra guidelines in felt pen to match the guidelines you have

worked on the fabric. Some people like to use magnetic markers
to identify the area of the chart they are working on. A thin
metal sheet is placed behind the page and magnetic locating
bars on the front are moved about as you progress. They can be
used in the book as well. As a general rule I start embroidering
at the centre and work blocks of colour at a time. Although this
book is devoted to cross stitch, the charts could also be used for
canvaswork (needlepoint) embroidery. Simply use half cross
stitch or tent stitch instead of whole cross stitch. Remember
you will then need to add a background colour to most of
the designs.

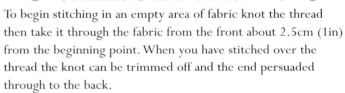

STARTING AND FINISHING

To begin stitching in an empty area of fabric knot the thread
then take it through the fabric from the front about 2.5cm (1in)
from the beginning point. When you have stitched over the
thread the knot can be trimmed off and the end persuaded
through to the back.

To start a new thread in a stitched area, just use the needle
to thread it under four or five stitches on the back of the work
before beginning to stitch.

To finish off, thread your needle back through the last four
or five stitches on the wrong side of the fabric and trim the
excess thread.

WASHING AND IRONING

If you have to wash a piece of embroidery use a mild detergent
well dissolved in hot water. Wash thoroughly without rubbing
and rinse until the stain disappears. Never leave the embroidery
wet. Remove excess water by rolling the item in a towel and
squeezing gently. Dry it flat then iron it from the back whilst
still damp.

Careful pressing will smooth the fabric and correct any
distortion without flattening the stitches and spoiling the
texture. Lay the embroidery face down on a thick towel covered
with a piece of sheet. Pull it into shape, making sure the fabric
grain is straight. Press gently on the back at a heat suitable for
the type of fabric and thread. Do not use steam on metallic
threads and cover the piece with a pressing cloth. Cottons
embroidered on Aida or cotton cloth can be pressed at the
two- to three-spot setting; anything involving synthetic fabric
or thread requires a cooler one-spot setting.

STITCHES

There are very few stitches required to complete the projects in this book – cross stitch, of course, plus some backstitch, long stitch and satin stitch. Some projects also have the addition of beads or sequins.

❧ BACKSTITCH ❧

This is an easy outline stitch that is used in some projects. The project instructions say whether it should be worked with one or two strands of cotton (floss). It is usually worked after the cross stitch over the same unit of fabric (one block or two threads) as you have used for the cross stitch. Follow the diagram below, first bringing the needle through the fabric from the back. Take a stitch backwards. Bring the needle up again at the far end of the next stitch along the line. Take another stitch backwards to fill in the gap.

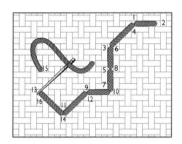

Backstitch

❧ CROSS STITCH ❧

This is the basic stitch used throughout this book. Either work individual crosses, or work half crosses along a line, then return, stitching over the half crosses in the opposite direction. The first method is the most stable and unlikely to cause distortion and so is perhaps to be preferred if working without a frame. Either is suitable, as long as you develop an even tension without pulling the stitch so tightly that it distorts the threads of the fabric. Choose which direction your top stitch will go and stick to it otherwise the texture will be uneven. The designs in this book use whole cross stitches and no fractional stitches. The diagrams below show how to work cross stitch over one block of Aida or over two threads of evenweave.

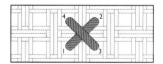

Cross stitch on Aida

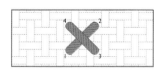

Cross stitch on evenweave

❧ DOUBLE RUNNING STITCH ❧

This stitch, which is also called Holbein stitch, is the traditional stitch for creating blackwork patterns. Follow the diagram below, working a row of running stitches in one direction, over and under two threads of evenweave or one block of Aida. Then work back the row in the opposite direction, filling in the gaps.

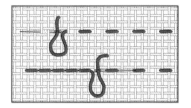

Double running stitch

❧ LADDER STITCH ❧

This is a neat way of joining the edges of two pieces of fabric that have already been neatened or have turnings. Follow the diagram below, bringing the needle out through the edge at one side and straight across into the other edge. Slip the needle through the edge a little way and take a stitch back to the first side, making another rung on the 'ladder'. Repeat as shown.

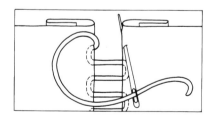

Ladder stitch

❧ SATIN STITCH ❧

This is a long stitch often worked in blocks to fill shapes. It has been used in the whitework section of the band sampler on page 26. It can be worked diagonally, horizontally or vertically. Follow the numbered sequence in the diagrams, laying the stitches flat, side by side, and taking care not to pull them too tightly.

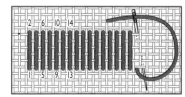 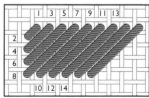

Satin stitch

MAKING UP

This section describes how to make up the projects as they are shown in the book, but as the designs are very adaptable, you could make them up in many other ways.

USING FUSIBLE INTERFACING

Fusible (iron-on) interfacing is very useful for small projects where the fabric needs to be trimmed to fit or if there is no room for turnings, for example, a bowl lid, paperweight or card. It is available in white and black for light or dark projects. Once ironed on it stabilizes the threads of the fabric, allowing the exact shape to be cut out without fear of fraying. Always press the embroidery before adding the interfacing. Try a small sample on the fabric you are using first.

MOUNTING WORK IN CARDS

There are many ready-made card mounts available today from various outlets. If desired, you can back the embroidery with fusible interfacing first (see above). Check your design fits the card aperture, trim the embroidery to slightly larger than the aperture and then attach it to the inside of the aperture with double-sided adhesive tape or craft glue. Stick the card flap on to the back of the embroidery, using more tape or glue.

STRETCHING AND FRAMING WORK

To make your work up into a framed picture you can simply press it and take it to a framer specializing in embroidery. If you prefer to do the mounting and framing yourself the following instructions should help. When framing behind a mount (mat) I sometimes just stick the embroidery to the backing card round the edges (though never allow glue on an area where it could be seen as a stain can develop over time). You could also try the adhesive boards available now for embroidery.

STRETCHING If an embroidery is to be framed without a mount it will need to be stretched over a piece of stiff card (often called mount board). This method can also be used to cure wrinkles or distortions. Use white card for pale fabrics and dark card for darker designs.

1 Cut the card to fit inside the picture frame, allowing for the thickness of fabric over the edges. Mark the centre of each side on the back of the card and mark where you want the centre of the embroidery to be. Lay the front of the card on the wrong side of the fabric, matching the centre marks.

2 Fold the fabric over the thick card and hold it in place by pushing pins into the card edges (see diagram below). Start at the centres and work outwards on opposite sides. Check that the fabric is held taut and that the grain is straight.

3 Take a long length of buttonhole or linen thread and lace from side to side, pulling the thread tightly enough to hold the fabric firmly in place without bending the card. Repeat this operation with the other two sides, then remove pins.

Lacing

FRAMING Today there are many outlets selling ready-made frames so you should have plenty of choice. I prefer to frame without glass, but if you do use glass make sure the embroidery isn't squashed up against the glass, flattening its texture. Use narrow strips of card at the edges of the frame, between the glass and the embroidery, to hold them apart. Clean both sides of the glass and then assemble the mounted embroidery in the frame.

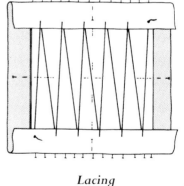

❀ MITRING A CORNER ❀

This is a neat way of removing excess fabric from a corner and is a good way to finish napkins and similar items. Fold the fabric in the required amount, mark the fold line and then unfold the turnings. At the corner, fold the fabric on the diagonal as shown in the diagram below and press the crease. Allowing for a small turning along the creased side, trim away the excess fabric. Turn in the long edges and the creased diagonal sides should meet in a neat mitre. Stitch them together invisibly.

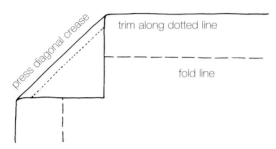

Mitring a corner

❀ MAKING UP A BELL PULL ❀

Many cross stitch designs look very attractive mounted on brass or wooden bell-pull ends – see page 102 for suppliers.

1 On the back of the embroidery, mark the edges of your bell pull – this will depend on the bell-pull ends you have chosen. If using a cord with a tape edging to finish the sides, position this next, tacking (basting) it in place before stitching it to the embroidered fabric along the marked edges.

2 Cut a piece of interfacing (such as stiff pelmet Vilene) to fit inside the marked area and position it to back the area that will be visible. Fold the long edges of the embroidery over it. Cut a piece of backing fabric slightly larger than the bell pull and fold over the long edges so it fit neatly on the back of the bell pull. Tack (baste) in place and stitch to the bell pull by hand.

3 Now attach the embroidery to the bell-pull ends. If you have used ends with a bar, fold the fabric round the bar. Decide how long the fold-back needs to be before trimming and neatening the ends and stitching in place over the bar at the back.

❀ MAKING A BOOK COVER ❀

These instructions apply to the heartsease book cover on page 8. Read through all the instructions first to understand what the end result will be.

1 Measure from the opening edge of your book, round the spine to the other edge. Cut a piece of fusible interfacing this length x the height of the book (see diagram below) and bond it to the back of the fabric. Wrap the fabric round the front cover, the spine and the back cover. On the insides of the covers the fabric should come to within about 1.25cm (½in) of the spine. Check this measurement on your book to find the length of the strip and add a little ease at the top and bottom of the height of the book to allow for the thickness of the covers.

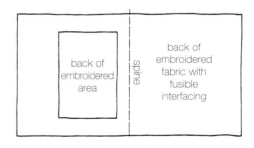

Making a book cover

2 Turn in the top and bottom edges of the fabric and neaten the ends. Wrap around the book to check the fit and then ladder stitch (see page 98) along at the top and bottom to form the two pockets for the front and back covers (see diagram below).

3 Open the book and pull the covers back. Fold the embroidered cover inside out and slip the book covers into the pockets. It should be a close fit, but not so tight that the book will not close completely.

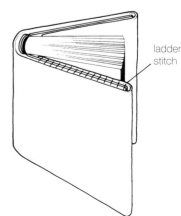

Wrapping the cover around the book

❀ MOUNTING WORK IN A BOX LID ❀

To mount embroidery in a box top, you could leave the guidelines in the fabric temporarily to help position the embroidery over the pad. Stretch over the pad as you would over card for a picture, using linen thread (see page 99). Remove the guidelines after stretching is complete.

❀ MAKING UP A CUSHION ❀

Many of the designs in the book would make wonderful cushions. The following instructions are for making a square or rectangular cushion. If making a circular cushion, follow the same instructions but use a circular template to help you to pin the pieces together neatly. Once finished, you could add cord or piping round the cushion edges.

1 On the embroidery, mark exactly where you want the edge to be, bearing in mind the size of cushion pad you are using. Choose a backing fabric that matches the embroidered fabric or tones with it and cut this to the finished size plus turnings.
2 Pin the embroidery and the backing fabric right sides together. With the wrong side of the embroidered fabric up, machine stitch around the edges following the marked line. Start a little way from one corner, go round three sides and finish by stitching a little way round the last corner, leaving a gap to put the pad through. Work another line of stitching round the corners to reinforce them.
3 Cut diagonally across the corners, quite close to the stitching, and trim the other edges leaving a usual seam allowance (see diagram above top right). Turn the cushion to the right side and press the seam. Insert the cushion pad and neatly slipstitch the gap closed. An alternative method is to make up the cushion with a backing piece with a zip inserted (see diagram above right). To do this use a slightly larger backing piece, cut in half. Place the two halves right sides together. Sew 5cm (2in) of the seam at the top and bottom and insert a zip in the gap. Proceed as above but do not leave a gap. Open the zip to turn the cushion and insert the pad. This method is recommended for circular cushions.

Making a cushion cover

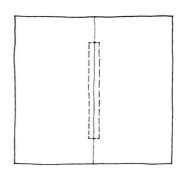

Back of cushion cover with a zip inserted

❀ MAKING A PINCUSHION ❀

Making up a pincushion (or a scissor keeper) is very similar to creating a cushion cover.

1 Mark out the finished size of the pincushion, add a turning allowance and trim away excess fabric.
2 Select and cut out an identically sized piece of fabric for the backing. If using a braid with a tape edging, position it with the braid on the inside of the stitching line and the tape towards the edge. Tack (baste) in place.
3 Pin the embroidery and backing together with right sides facing. With matching sewing thread, stitch round three sides, continuing a little way round into the fourth side. Turn right side out, fill with polyester stuffing and slipstitch the gap to complete.
4 Add tassels if desired. To make a tassel, wind a long length of stranded cotton (floss) around a small piece of stiff card. Slide the bundle of threads off the card, wind a short length of thread around the neck of the tassel and tie off. Cut across the ends of the tassel neatly

SUPPLIERS

DMC THREADS & ZWEIGART FABRICS
DMC Creative World Ltd
Pullman Road, Wigston,
Leicestershire LE18 2DY, UK
tel: 0116 2811040
fax: 0116 2813592
www.dmc.com

DMC Corporation
10 Port Kearny, South Kearny,
NJ 07032-4612, USA
tel: 973 5898931
www.dmc.com *or* www.zweigart.com

DMC
Radda Pty Ltd
51–55 Carrington Rd, Marrickville,
New South Wales 2204, Australia
tel: 0295 593088
email: info@radda.com.au

Craft & Co
PO Box 8086, Riccarton, Christchurch
8034, New Zealand
tel: 6433398230
email: info@wtc.co.nz

Willow Fabrics (mail order)
95 Town Lane, Mobberley,
Cheshire WA16 7HH, UK
tel: 0800 0567811
www.willowfabrics.com

Fabric Flair
For suppliers ask at your local craft store or
www.fabricflair.com

MCG Textiles Inc
www.mcgtextiles.com

**ANCHOR STRANDED COTTONS, OPHIR
AND KREINIK METALLIC THREADS**
From Coats Crafts stockists:
Coats Crafts UK
PO Box 22, McMullen Rd,
Darlington, County Durham
DL1 1YQ, UK
tel: 01325 392437
www.coatscrafts.co.uk

Coats North America
3430 Torrington Way, Suite 301, Charlotte
NC 28277, US
tel: +1704 3295800
fax: +1704 3295820
www.coatscna.com

Coats and Clark
Greenville, SC 29612 0229, USA
tel: 800 243 08 10
fax: 864 877 61 17

Semco Crafts
Unit 4, 7–11 Paraweena Road, Taren Point,
Sydney, NSW 2229, Australia
tel: 612 9525 4300
www.semco.com.au

Semco Crafts
PO Box 258040, 33C Sir William Avenue,
East Tamaki, Auckland 1730, New Zealand
tel: 649 273 8040
fax: 649 273 8041

Kreinik Manufacturing Co Inc
3106 Lord Baltimore Drive, Suite 101,
Baltimore, MD 21244, USA
tel: 1 800 537 2166
www.kreinik.com

MADEIRA THREADS
www.madeira.co.uk

Also from craft shops or mail order from:
Barnyarns Ltd
www.barnyarns.com

UK Freepost NEA12381, York YO51 9NS
tel: 0870 8708586

Brickyard Road, Boroughbridge, North
Yorkshire YO51 9NS, UK
tel: +44 1423 326423

Madeira (USA) Ltd
PO Box 6068, 30 Bayside Court,
Laconia, NH03246800-225-3001, USA
tel: 603 5282944
www.madeirausa.com

EBONY SILK THREADS
Leon Conrad Designs Ltd
20 Courtenay Street,
London SE11 5PQ, UK
tel: 020 7582 8213
fax: 020 7793 8339
www.leonconraddesigns.freeserve.co.uk
(For the blackwork box lid)

SEQUINS AND BEADS
Golden Threads
Brimstone Cottage, Pounsley Mill,
Blackboys, East Sussex, TN22 5HS, UK
tel/fax: 01825 831815
www.goldenthreads.co.uk
(For small sequins)

The London Bead Company
339, Kentish Town Road, London NW5 2TJ
tel: 020 7267 9413
fax: 020 7284 2062
www.londonbeadco.co.uk
(For small sequins)

MILL HILL BEADS
www.millhill.com
From **Framecraft Miniatures Ltd**
Litchfield Road, Brownhills, Walsall, West
Midlands WS8 6LH, UK
tel/fax: 01543 360842

Gay Bowles Sales Inc
PO Box 1060, Janesville, WI 53547, USA
tel: 608 754 9212
fax: 608 754 0665

Ireland Needlecraft
PO Box 1175, Narre Warren 3805
Victoria, Australia
tel: +61 0397023222

ACCESSORIES
Framecraft Miniatures Ltd as before
(For trinket pots, coasters and wooden poles)

Fabric Flair
www.fabricflair.com
(For large coasters)

The Viking Loom
22 High Petergate, York, YO1 7EH, UK
tel/fax: 01904 765599
www.vikingloom.co.uk
(For circular knot box, brass bell-pull ends)

Riverbank Woodcrafts
Unit 2B, Drum Industrial Estate,
Chester-le-Street, Co. Durham, DH2 1AG, UK
tel: 0191 3889673
www.riverbank-woodcrafts.co.uk
(For wooden boxes)

**Peter Hodson Quality Picture Frames
and Gallery**
44–48 Coronation Road, Cleethorpes,
North East Lincolnshire DN35 8RS, UK
tel/fax: 01472 604853
(For brass firescreen accessories – feet and
handle to fit on a picture frame)

Craft Creations
Ingersoll House, Delamere Road, Cheshunt,
Hertfordshire EN8 9HD, UK
tel: 01992 781900
www.craftcreations.com
(For card mounts)

Note from the author
Every effort is made to check that the fabrics
used in projects continue to be available
from their manufacturers. However, should
any become unavailable, check my website
where a whole page is devoted to fabrics,
and I can recommend alternatives.
www.wessexcollection.co.uk

ACKNOWLEDGMENTS

I am particularly grateful to all the embroiderers who have helped me by stitching samples for the photographs. They are all so skilful and reliable and have done a marvellous job.
I particularly want to thank:
Jennifer Bishop for the peascod and honeysuckle picture;
Stephanie Bramwell for the marigold cushion;
Muriel Gray for the gilliflower bag, the rose and thistle picture and the strawberry pincushion;
Joan Harris for the holly and acorn cushions, the stag bag and the Sheldon tapestry cushion;
Kay King for the heartsease bookmark;
Kate Lydford for the Tudor garden box lid;
Shirley Morris for the heart box lid;
Llyn Parker for the blackwork box lid;
Valerie Ray for the bluebell cushion and the bird and borage picture;
Carole Smith for the Sheldon bell pull;
Paula Tuckey for the heartsease book cover and the bountiful tree firescreen.

Many companies have been very helpful and generous in providing materials and accessories: my thanks to DMC for fabrics and threads and to Cara for her advice; to Coats for Coats and Kreinik metallic threads; to Framecraft for accessories including the decorative pot and the sampler accessories and the Mill Hill beads; to Craft Creations for card mounts.

My thanks to my commissioning editor, Cheryl Brown and editor Jennifer Proverbs, executive art editor Ali Myer and art editor Prudence Rogers, and a big thank you to Lin Clements for her hard work getting the text and charts into shape. Thanks also to the photographers Kim Sayer, Lucy Mason and Karl Adamson. And to all my family for all their help and support.

ABOUT THE AUTHOR

Barbara Hammet is a designer who began her career teaching art and crafts and art history. Her interests then turned to embroidery, attracted by the colours and textures of fabrics and threads, and she now runs an established design business, Wessex Collection Embroidery, selling kits based on historic designs. She has already had three books published by David & Charles: *The Art of William Morris in Cross Stitch*, *Art Nouveau Cross Stitch* and *Celtic Art in Cross Stitch*. Barbara lives in the city of Winchester in Hampshire, UK.

BIBLIOGRAPHY

ARTHUR, Liz *Embroidery 1600–1700 at the Burrell Collection*
(John Murray, 1995)

BECK, Thomasina *Embroidered Gardens* (Angus and Robertson, 1979)

BECK, Thomasina *The Embroiderer's Flowers* (David & Charles, 1992)

BECK, Thomasina *The Embroiderer's Story: Needlework from the
Renaissance to the Present Day* (David & Charles, 1995)

BENN Elizabeth (ed.) *Treasures from the Embroiderers' Guild Collection*
(David & Charles, 1991)

BROWN, Clare and WEARDON, Jennifer *Samplers from the
Victoria and Albert Museum* (V&A, 1999)

COLBY, Averil *Samplers* (Batsford, 1987)

DIGBY, George Wingfield *Elizabethan Embroidery*
(Faber and Faber, 1963)

DORE, Judith *Needlework and Tapestry at Parham Park*
(Parham Park Publications, 1993)

KING, Donald and LEVEY, Santina *Embroidery in Britain from
1200–1750* (V&A, 1993)

LEVEY, Santina M. *The Elizabethan Inheritance – the Hardwick Hall
Textiles* (The National Trust, 1998)

MAYOR, Susan and FOWLE, Diana *Samplers* (Studio Editions, 1990)

Le MOYNE DE MORGUES, Jacques (1533–88) *Portraits of Plants*
(V&A)

SWAIN, Margaret *The Needlework of Mary, Queen of Scots*
(Ruth Bean, 1986)

SYNGE, Lanto *The Art of Embroidery: The Royal School of Needlework –
a History of Style and Design* (Antique Collectors' Club, 2001)

WHALLEY, Robin and JENNINGS, Anne *Knot Gardens and Parterres*
(Barn Elms, 1998)

A Schole-house for the Needle (first published 1632, reprinted 1998
MJL Smith & Associates)

INDEX